# INSIDE

## THE

# INSURANCE INDUSTRY

*What you don't know WILL hurt you!*

### Kevin L. Glaser
**CPCU, CIC, SCLA, ARM, AAI, AIC, ARM-P, AIS**

**Third Edition**

ISBN 978-0-9910388-1-7

Library of Congress Control Number: 2014901559

Cover artwork by Briana R. Glaser
Cover and interior design by Sarah White

**Limit of Liability/Disclaimer of Warranty:**

# Contents

Acknowledgements . . . . . . . . . . . . . . . . . . . . . . . . . . . . . . . . . . . . . v

Prologue . . . . . . . . . . . . . . . . . . . . . . . . . . . . . . . . . . . . . . . . . . viii

1. How Insurance Companies Work . . . . . . . . . . . . . . . . . . . . . . 1

2. Insurance Company Internal Department Functions. . . . . . . . 8
   Marketing . . . . . . . . . . . . . . . . . . . . . . . . . . . . . . . . . . . . .8
   Claims. . . . . . . . . . . . . . . . . . . . . . . . . . . . . . . . . . . . . . .14
   Underwriting . . . . . . . . . . . . . . . . . . . . . . . . . . . . . . . . .26
   Policy Services. . . . . . . . . . . . . . . . . . . . . . . . . . . . . . . . .28
   Audit Department. . . . . . . . . . . . . . . . . . . . . . . . . . . . . .28
   Loss Control . . . . . . . . . . . . . . . . . . . . . . . . . . . . . . . . . .30

3. Other Insurance Company Support Positions . . . . . . . . . . . . 33
   Legal . . . . . . . . . . . . . . . . . . . . . . . . . . . . . . . . . . . . . . .33
   Actuary . . . . . . . . . . . . . . . . . . . . . . . . . . . . . . . . . . . . .35
   Subrogation. . . . . . . . . . . . . . . . . . . . . . . . . . . . . . . . . .38
   Internal Audit . . . . . . . . . . . . . . . . . . . . . . . . . . . . . . . .40
   Product Development . . . . . . . . . . . . . . . . . . . . . . . . . . .41
   Information Technology . . . . . . . . . . . . . . . . . . . . . . . . .42
   Management. . . . . . . . . . . . . . . . . . . . . . . . . . . . . . . . . .44

4. A Little Known Factor Affecting Insurance Companies . . . . . 49

    Reinsurance. . . . . . . . . . . . . . . . . . . . . . . . . . . . . . . . . . .49

5. Pricing. . . . . . . . . . . . . . . . . . . . . . . . . . . . . . . . . . . . . . . . . 54

6. External (Third Party) Resources. . . . . . . . . . . . . . . . . . . . . . 61

    Public Adjusters. . . . . . . . . . . . . . . . . . . . . . . . . . . . . . . .61

    Insurance Consultants. . . . . . . . . . . . . . . . . . . . . . . . . . .62

    Exposure Analysis and Recommendations . . . . . . . . . .63

    Other Specialized Services . . . . . . . . . . . . . . . . . . . . . .64

7. Insurance Litigation . . . . . . . . . . . . . . . . . . . . . . . . . . . . . . 65

    Bad Faith. . . . . . . . . . . . . . . . . . . . . . . . . . . . . . . . . . . .67

    Sample Engagements. . . . . . . . . . . . . . . . . . . . . . . . . . .70

8. How to Get the Best Insurance "Deal" . . . . . . . . . . . . . . . . . 72

9. Risk Management . . . . . . . . . . . . . . . . . . . . . . . . . . . . . . . . . 79

10. The Future of Insurance . . . . . . . . . . . . . . . . . . . . . . . . . . . 85

Epilogue . . . . . . . . . . . . . . . . . . . . . . . . . . . . . . . . . . . . . . . . . 89

Appendix. . . . . . . . . . . . . . . . . . . . . . . . . . . . . . . . . . . . . . . . . 91

    Sample Risk Management Case Study. . . . . . . . . . . . .91

INDEX. . . . . . . . . . . . . . . . . . . . . . . . . . . . . . . . . . . . . . . . . . 101

About the Author . . . . . . . . . . . . . . . . . . . . . . . . . . . . . . . . . 108

# Acknowledgements

There are a great many people who deserve my thanks and appreciation for providing guidance and assistance to me throughout my professional career. However, there are none more deserving of my endearing gratitude than my immediate family.

More than twenty years ago my wife, my 2-year-old son and I moved several hundred miles from our hometown to Wisconsin. We left behind friends and family for a new adventure and had no one to rely upon but ourselves. First and foremost, I wish to thank my wonderful wife, Patty, for all of the support she has given to me throughout our 30 years of marriage. She willingly moved to a new home in a faraway state, encouraged me to start an insurance and risk management consulting business from scratch, and has been the rock upon whom I have leaned for so many years. She continues to be the person I rely upon more than anyone else, and I am blessed to have her in my life.

I am also grateful to my oldest son, Nick, for the many special talents that he shares with me and the rest of our family. Nick is a young professional in the insurance industry and is learning as much as he can about his chosen career. Nick provided the impetus for me to publish my initial edition of Inside the Insurance Industry and without him, that book would never have been published.

Many thanks to my second son, Greg, for providing several helpful insights during his tenure at my consulting business over summer months. Greg has the ability to look at things many different ways and provided me with valuable input as a result. He also has chosen the insurance industry as his career and has mapped out his plan for future success in this business.

Becky, my oldest daughter, adds perspectives outside the realm of insurance and deserves my thanks and gratitude as a result of her many talents that she shares with me and our family. She is a talented singer, musician, actress and caregiver, and she manages to achieve outstanding grades while on her path to obtain a nursing degree. Her various involvements allow me to step outside of the insurance and risk management world and helps to remind me of the importance of staying well-rounded in life.

And last, I am thankful to my youngest child, Briana, for her quick wit, natural intelligence, musical skills, and "fun to be with" personality. She has earned respected community-wide awards for her many good works throughout the Oconomowoc area, and Briana's extra-curricular activities make me proud that she is thinking of so many others at her young age. Briana also possesses artistic abilities as evidenced by this book's cover artwork.

# Prologue

In my more than twenty-five years spent working in various capacities within the insurance industry, I have witnessed many changes. One thing that has not changed is the confusion surrounding insurance products that are sold to customers. The operative word in the last sentence is "sold."

It continues to amaze me how little individuals and decision-makers at businesses know about the insurance products that they purchase. Thousands of dollars, hundreds of thousands of dollars and even more than one million dollars may be spent to buy property and casualty insurance policies, yet buyers do not understand what they are spending money on. Insurance is sold and decisions are made based upon factors such as the insurance agent's looks, his presentation abilities, the relationships between parties, and so forth. Yet, these things have little to do with the true reason insurance should be bought.

Insurance is a contract between the insurance company and the individual or business that purchases its product — the insurance policy. The insurance policy promises to reimburse you (property losses) or pay on your behalf (liability losses) if a specific occurrence takes place that is covered under the policy — subject to conditions, limitations and exclusions. Therefore, it is imperative that buyers of insurance understand how insurance companies work, how insurance products are developed, how insurance is sold, how claims are handled, the insured's (you are the insured) legal rights under the insurance policy and more.

I understand that most people do not want to spend a lot of time thinking about the topic of insurance. However, by taking a "head in the sand" approach, the consumer allows insurance companies complete control over every aspect of the insurance process, and this need not be the case.

It is in your best interest to educate yourself in the area of insurance. No matter how much money you pay for insurance it is likely a high percentage of your overall budget. Know what you are getting for your money and understand the rights you are afforded under the insurance contract.

My intent in writing this book is to share with you the inner workings of insurance companies. As a result you will be able to make educated insurance purchasing decisions, and you will gain a better understanding of how you can proactively address issues that may arise within the provisions of your insurance policies.

# INSIDE

## THE

# INSURANCE INDUSTRY

*What you don't know WILL hurt you!*

# 1

## How Insurance Companies Work

Most people don't understand how insurance companies operate. During a recent court case in which I provided expert testimony, a great deal of my time was spent helping the jury understand how insurance company operating structures work. The jury was made up of twelve individuals from every walk of life. There were students, housewives, business people, retirees and others. The one common thread was that none of them really understood even the most basic concepts about insurance.

Part of my job was to help the jury understand the insurance company distribution process, among other things. To accomplish this, I used a flip chart and compared an auto manufacturer to an insurance company.

In essence, insurance companies (also known as "insurers," "carriers" and "primary insurers") are much like car manufacturers. Both sell final products to consumers — one sells automobiles and the other insurance policies. Some common characteristics include:

each industry has Product Development Departments, both keep their eyes on competitors and make product changes accordingly, and each is subject to government regulation.

Other similarities between auto manufacturers and insurance companies will be shared throughout this book to help you better understand the insurance industry.

As a starting point, understand that insurance companies are typically chartered as *mutual* or *stock* companies. A mutual company is owned by its policyholders (also referred to as "insureds"). A stock company is owned by its stockholders. There are pros and cons to each type of company charter.

The main advantage of a **mutual** company from an insurance consumer's perspective is the possibility of receiving a "refund" in the form of a policy dividend if the insurance company's profit-making results are better than anticipated. In other words, if the company makes money based upon the rate (price) it charges, after paying claims and other expenses, it can refund a portion of these profits to its policyholders. Such refunds may take the form of rate *reductions* or *maintaining current insurance product pricing*.

Realistically, while the mutual companies tout their structure and claim that their ability to reduce prices is a result of being owned by their policyholders, the prices they charge for their products are seldom lower than the prices charged by other types of insurance companies when comparisons are made on an "apples to apples" basis.

The main advantage of **stock** companies is that they do tend to be priced very competitively up front because they are encouraged to make a profit for their stockholders. Profits that are realized are typically paid out to the stockholders not the insurance policyholders. Stock companies have an additional advantage in that they can sell more stock if they need to raise capital for any reason. Over the years, a number of mutual companies have converted to stock companies in order to acquire other companies, to expand their product offerings and to grow the geographical territories in which they were conducting business.

Insurance companies can also be distinguished by the type of product **distribution method** they use. The three main distribution methods are: through an *independent agency*, through an *exclusive agency*, or through a *direct writer*.

In the **independent agency system**, agents sell the products of many different insurance companies. Basically, these agencies are individually-owned, profit-oriented businesses, much like a local appliance store that sells several different manufacturer brand names. In reality these independent agencies act as "manufacturer's representatives" for insurance companies.

Using the auto manufacturer analogy, car makers distribute their products through auto dealerships. Each dealership is individually owned and may sell various brands of cars. Manufacturers and dealerships enter into contracts that detail the responsibilities of each party and manufacturers offer dealerships the opportunity to earn bonuses based upon sales numbers. All of these characteristics also hold true for insurance companies and the agencies that operate within the independent agency system.

Independent insurance agents advertise individually, as part of trade associations like the Professional Insurance Agents (PIA) and under the marketing umbrella of the insurance carriers they represent. Usually, the insurance agent and the insurance company share the cost of advertising. This type of arrangement is known as cooperative advertising, or "co-op advertising." An example of this type of arrangement is an insurance agency that represents and sells insurance for CNA or Chubb.

Alternatively, **exclusive agents** (also referred to as "Captive Agents") must place business with only one insurance company (referred to as the "Captive Company"), but often have the flexibility to run their offices as they see fit. Agents who exclusively represent one insurance company may be considered *independent contractors* by the insurance company (e.g. American Family Insurance) or they may be considered *employees* (e.g. State Farm and Liberty Mutual). Many exclusive agents are restricted by contract from submitting business to any other company unless the application is first rejected by the agent's captive company.

For exclusive agencies, the marketing of insurance products is typically the responsibility of the insurance company, although exclusive agents can also mount their own marketing campaigns in order to gain name recognition in their communities.

Yet another method of insurance distribution involves **direct writers**. Here, insurance is sold by an *employee* of an insurance company and *all* business must be written exclusively with that insurer. The policies sold by employee agents are owned by these insurance companies. Therefore, when employee agents leave, they are not entitled to take the insurance policy (or the customer) with them.

In order to market their insurance products, many direct writing companies use *television* and *print advertising, telephone, web-related* or *mail solicitation* to sell their insurance products to the public. Many times, direct writers will combine several different sales methods to market their products. Examples of direct writer insurance companies include GEICO and USAA.

Regardless of who pays for it, the marketing of insurance products has changed over the past several years and it is constantly evolving. For example, *telephone marketing* was prevalent in the past. But with the advent of "do not call" lists in several states, insurance companies are now focusing on other methods. *Internet marketing* has seen exponential growth. Almost unheard of a few years ago, things such as blogs, website enhancements (including the tracking of visitors), twitter postings (tweets), Facebook and the use of other types of social media have become commonplace. Some companies are even testing the sending of targeted cell phone advertisements to potential insurance customers.

Insurance agents, themselves, are also using the internet in a variety of ways in order to generate new leads, and hopefully, new sales.

Before leaving the area of insurance product distribution, it is critical that a frequent cause of consumer confusion be made clear. Some insurance agents refer to themselves as insurance agents and others refer to themselves as insurance brokers. What is the difference?

**Insurance agents** have signed contracts to represent insurance companies and to sell the products offered by these insurance companies. As a result, legally, they have a *dual fiduciary responsibility* to both the insurance companies they represent and to the customers that buy the insurance policies that they sell.

**Insurance brokers** technically represent their *customers*, not insurance companies. While there remains a *legal* differentiation between insurance agents and insurance brokers, in practical terms there is no difference. Insurance brokers today have signed contracts in effect with a multitude of insurance companies, just as independent insurance agents do.

Examples of insurance *brokers* include Aon, Marsh USA and A.J. Gallagher & Co. Some well-known larger insurance *agencies* include SIAA (Hampton, NH), Lockton Companies (Kansas City, MO) and Mesirow Financial (Chicago, IL).

Please note that the words "agent" and "broker" will be used interchangeably in this book since both terms refer to a representative who sells for an insurance company.

The insurance business came under scrutiny several years ago when Eliot Spitzer, then the State of New York's Attorney General, investigated a case of **bid-rigging**. The situation in Mr. Spitzer's case involved a large insurance brokerage that was controlling *which* insurance companies would provide bids, as well as the *prices* that the insurance companies would charge for the coverages requested. In direct conflict with a broker's legal duty to their customers, this brokerage acted in the best interest of the insurance company and itself. How? The insurance brokerage was positioning itself to receive the highest possible commissions from insurance companies by restricting the consumers' access to other insurance companies and/or by increasing the prices consumers paid. As a result of the Attorney General's investigation, the area of contingent commissions in the insurance industry became a matter of public concern.

Auto makers often offer some type of bonus to dealerships that sell their cars. This may be in the form of a dealer holdback, or some other incentive. Likewise, insurance companies pay contingent commissions not only to insurance brokers, but agents as well, on an annual basis, predicated upon their performance during the prior twelve-month period. These commissions are paid when certain specific criteria are met. These criteria generally include things such as:

- Monetary growth (measured by insurance policies sold)
- Number growth (growth on a "per policy" basis compared to last year)
- Loss ratio results (dollars paid out in claims divided by the amount of money paid for an insurance policy. Typically, a pure loss ratio of less than 50% is desirable)
- Policy retention percentages (how many policies an insurance agent kept at the date the insurance renewed. A number higher than 80% is decent)

- Miscellaneous other factors, such as a block of insurance policies moved from one insurance carrier to another (known as a "book of business rollover"); premium growth in specific industries or at specific agency office locations, etc.

As a result of public backlash, several large insurance agencies and brokers (but not all of them) decided to no longer accept contingent commissions. Today, many of the agencies and brokers that refused to accept contingent commissions have re-evaluated this position and now once again accept these payments. The reasoning behind their change of heart differs, but some agencies felt that as long as they fully disclose their potential to obtain contingent commission income (what they consider "transparency"), it was acceptable to once again enter into some type of additional commission agreements with insurance carriers. Other insurance agencies and brokers never did stop taking bonus commission dollars and continued to accept these "enhanced commissions" from insurance carriers with the blessing of their customers. Many other consumers, though, remained unaware of this potential conflict of interest and how it might affect the cost of their insurance.

An important caveat to purchasers of insurance: the bid-rigging type of situation that was exposed by Eliot Spitzer in the past is still a concern today. Part of the reason for this is the insurance placement process itself. Agents and brokers continue to be in control of which insurance companies are involved in the insurance bidding process. In addition, they present the ultimate insurance proposal (coverages and prices) to their customers.

# 2

**Insurance Company Internal Department Functions**

It is important to have at least a basic understanding of the way insurance companies do business because any one of the departments may have an adverse impact on the insurance policy that you have purchased.

The **major internal departments** in insurance companies are: *Marketing, Claims, Underwriting, Policy Services, Audit Department* and *Loss Control*. Other **support positions** include: *Legal, Actuary, Subrogation, Internal Audit, Product Development, Information Technology* and *Management*. Each of these departments will be discussed separately, with other support positions addressed in chapter 3.

### Marketing

*Marketing* consists of both an *internal* and an *external* sales force. An *internal sales force* consists of the employees of the insurance company who "sell" to, or support, the company's chosen distribution channel. *External marketing* (or "sales force") sells the insurance company's products to the final customer via the individual company's chosen distribution channel. These distribution methods include independent agents, captive agents and direct sales.

The external sales force is composed of the independent agency or exclusive agency agents who sell the insurance company's products. These external salespersons are often categorized as "sales" rather than "marketing," but both are involved in the process of influencing the ultimate decision-maker, the consumer, to buy their company's insurance product. Note that the direct writer company's Marketing Department fulfills both internal and external sales functions.

If independent insurance agents are used, the insurance company's *marketing representatives* work to convince agents who have contracts with their company that they should be selling their company's products. Where captive or exclusive agents are used, *internal marketing* provides sales assistance to the individual agent — such as training; acting as a liaison between agents and the company to help when there is a problem, and assisting in writing new insurance policies — referred to as "new accounts."

Internal marketing also keeps others in the insurance company abreast of what competing companies are doing in the marketplace, and may provide assistance in development of new products or making changes to existing products.

There are pros and cons to each method of insurance sales from a customer's point of view. Even though independent agents tout the fact that they do not work for any single insurance company, and do, in fact, have a duty to work in the best interests of their customers, they also have a fiduciary (legal) duty to each of the companies that they represent. This sets the stage for possible conflicts of interest.

Agents who sell the products of one company — or exclusive agents — must sell whatever is available to them via that single company, no matter how costly, or how good or bad it is. Companies that have chosen this method of distribution typically put much more emphasis on the "sales" process. The people who sell their products are well-trained salespersons who know how to sell around all types of objections.

Interestingly, many insurance agents are people who were previously sports stars, or have otherwise been involved in activities that result in name recognition in the communities where they sell insurance. Consumers of insurance feel "special" when they rub elbows with these agents, and are proud to tell their friends and neighbors who they buy their insurance policies from.

If a person does not have a well-known public profile and wants to get into insurance sales, he or she must typically have somewhere between 100 to 1,000 *leads* to contact prior to starting an insurance sales career path because there is no consumer name recognition.

Once someone is hired as an insurance agent and the initial 100 to 1,000 leads have been exhausted, how can the agent generate additional leads? There are a number of methods. They can be *purchased from outside companies* who specialize in this sort of thing. They can come as a result of *advertising*. However, the most popular method is to develop and work off of a list of *referrals*. Referrals come about when a person or business seeks out an agent based on something positive they have heard about the person, or when one of the agent's existing customers provides the name of a friend or business associate to the agent. In a best-case scenario, the insurance agent's existing customers pave the way for the agent to contact their personal friends or business associates.

While this latter method is the most popular way of making insurance sales, it does *not* necessarily result in the best situation for the insurance consumer. Many times the power of a referral is so strong that the buyer asks very few important questions, such as those relating to the experience and qualifications of the person selling insurance policies (refer to the section, *"Some questions you should ask a prospective insurance agent"* found later in this book).

Incentives are often used by companies to generate activity (new business production) on the part of their agency sales force. Captive insurance companies appeal to their agents' desire for money and prestige (i.e., publishing their names in company-wide newsletters or making it to the top-tier "President's Club"), as well as continued employment. Independent insurance companies offer exotic trips (cruises, trips to Switzerland and Hong Kong, etc.) and additional commissions (over and above "contingent commissions" discussed earlier and below) for selling *their* products instead of a competitor's product. All of these incentives can adversely impact the type and amount of insurance you are sold, especially if you are unaware of them.

The issue of "contingent commissions" has been touched upon earlier. However, it merits further discussion. Remember, contingent commissions are *additional* commission dollars that are paid to agencies when certain, contractually agreed-upon criteria are met. Examples of when contingent commissions might be paid include:

- "x-amount" of new business production is written with an insurance company;
- "x-percentage" of profitability on the book of business that exists with the insurance company (usually determined by the *loss ratio* performance of the book of business); or
- a combination of these, or other criteria

These incentives are rarely, if ever, discussed with the purchaser of insurance policies. In some ways, contingent commissions are no different than bonuses paid in a variety of other industries based upon certain criteria stated in the contract between, for instance, a mortgage broker and the financial companies they represent, or a manufacturer and their manufacturer's representative for certain agreed-upon performance objectives.

However, there clearly is the possibility that an insurance agent is writing your insurance policy with an insurance company just to earn a better sales commission bonus — rather than because that is the best company for you to be written with. Make certain that your agent is not placing you with an insurance company to better the agent's own self-interest by specifically asking whether the agent receives additional compensation for selling a particular insurance policy to you.

Another situation that merits discussion is when an insurance agent is so focused on receiving a contingency payment from an insurance company that he or she will actually refuse to write insurance policies for some customers. For example, one of my clients manufactures agricultural machinery. Part of my annual project involves obtaining renewal insurance policy quotes to ascertain which insurance company can provide the best combination of coverages and pricing for the upcoming year.

I began my project by lining up the best insurance companies to insure my client, keeping in mind their specific business operations. One of the insurance companies appeared to be an excellent fit for my client's business — in fact several agents wanted this particular insurer assigned to them. I vetted each of the agents and decided to assign the insurer to the insurance agent who had the second-largest written premium with the insurance company in the state of Wisconsin. My intent was to have this agent leverage their carrier relationship to provide a very attractive quote to my client.

Towards the end of the project, just prior to the deadline given for insurance proposals, the agent who was assigned the preferred insurer told me that he did not want the insurance company to release a quote. Why? He said he was afraid that my client might have a claim after he wrote the insurance policy and that this would adversely impact the amount of contingency income that he had been receiving from the insurance carrier.

While this outcome was a surprise, remember that the insurance agent is an independent businessperson and is allowed to make decisions that he or she feel are in the best interest of their insurance agency. This includes areas such as profitability and which business customers they wish to insure. In my opinion, the significantly better course of action in this situation would have been for this insurance agent to decline to even get involved in the quote process for my client. If that had happened, another insurance agent would have had the opportunity to write my client's insurance with the very same insurance company.

Before leaving the area of insurance sales, it is worthwhile to note that in most states insurance agents legally owe minimal duties and responsibilities to their customers. In general, it is the duty of **buyers** of insurance to tell their insurance agent the *coverage* that they desire, as well as the *limit* of insurance that they want. The insurance buyer also has a duty to *read the policy* that they receive.

Insurance **sellers** (agents) are responsible for making certain that what the customer ordered was delivered by the insurance company, and often, little else. Insurance agent duties, however, can become broader depending on specific situations, such as when an insurance agent actively provides advice in a consultant-type role, where fees are received in addition to commissions, the length of time that the insurance customer and insurance agent relationship has been in existence, and so forth.

Many people are surprised by the limited legal duties imposed upon insurance agents. While at first blush this may not seem fair, you must understand that there are many opportunities for misunderstandings to arise during the insurance placement process. It is not at all uncommon for insurance purchasers to say (or to think that they have said) to their insurance agent, "I want coverage for everything." Of course, this is an impossible request.

My advice to insurance purchasers is to have their insurance agents acknowledge ***in writing*** any coverage that they feel is important, and to take the time to *very carefully* review any insurance applications prior to signing them. Ask questions if you are unclear about anything that pertains to the insurance policy you are purchasing. No one looks out for your best interests like you do.

## Claims

An insurance policy is nothing more (or less) than a contract. Here, the contract is a promise by the insurance company to pay if an "event" occurs that is covered under the terms of the contract. The **claims adjusters** are the ones who interpret whether or not a claim that is presented is an event that is covered under the policy (contract) purchased.

The *claims department* consists of adjusters who may work strictly *inside*, or who may work strictly *outside* (in the field), or a *combination* of the two. Simply put, adjusters are the people who control the insurance company's checkbook. Theirs is a difficult job because their company may criticize them for paying too much money on a claim, while their policyholders may criticize them for not paying enough!

**Know this**: Claims Adjusters have a fair amount of leeway in deciding how much money a policyholder or a claimant will ultimately be paid. The adjusters who excel in their positions are the ones who get claims closed while paying the least amount of money. Additional kudos is earned by keeping customers happy, but many times this is a secondary consideration.

An adjuster may, albeit infrequently, consult with an *underwriter* (refer to the **Underwriting** section for additional information about this position) for their "intent" concerning a specific insurance policy coverage provision, since underwriters are many times involved with drafting specific policy language. However, the ultimate decision whether or not to pay a claim lies with the adjuster. Most insurance companies follow ISO (Insurance Services Office), which promulgates the vast majority of insurance policy coverage language used by insurance companies today. Because of the wide use of specific insurance policy language, many insurance policy provisions are "court tested" and, as a result, case law exists for many coverage disputes. Adjusters use *case law, internal insurance company claims handling guidelines,* and other *reference/resource materials* when adjusting claims.

Adjusters become aware of case law from sources such as insurance company claims management, internal and external attorneys and from claims-focused magazines and periodicals. Reference materials that may be used by adjusters include items such as Fire, Casualty and Surety (FC&S) Bulletins; Insurance Services Office (ISO) ISOnet; National Council on Compensation Insurance (NCCI); the International Risk Management Institute (IRMI); National Underwriter; Rough Notes; the National Alliance For Insurance Education and Research; A.M. Best and a variety of other resources.

Insurance companies and their insurance adjusters do have specific duties they owe their policyholders. Many of these duties are contained in the NAIC (National Association of Insurance Commissioners) **Unfair Claims Settlement Practices Act Model** language. Provisions of this Act have been adopted as claims handling standards in legislation passed by several states.

The Unfair Claims Settlement Practices provisions provide standards that insurance companies should follow so that their insureds are treated fairly. The Act attempts to encourage insurance companies to handle claims promptly and to provide fair and equitable settlements between insurance companies and their claimants.

Examples of provisions that are contained in the Unfair Claims Settlement Practices Act Model include:

- Insurance companies must fully disclose all benefits and coverages in their customer's insurance policy.
- Insurance companies cannot misrepresent their policies.
- Insurance companies cannot deny a claim based on arbitrary time limits given to customers to prove their loss or property damage.
- Insurance companies must acknowledge claims "promptly" after the claim is filed. Note that States may define the word "promptly" in different ways, or not at all.
- Insurance companies must provide reasonable assistance during the claims process. This includes promptly supplying customers with appropriate forms and clear instructions.
- All claim investigations must take place in a reasonable amount of time.
- Insurance companies should not enter into settlement negotiations with a claimant who is not represented by an attorney or who is not an attorney.

- Insurance companies cannot send a settlement to a claimant that is less than the total cost of damages unless the customer agrees.
- Insurance companies cannot force you to travel an unreasonable distance during your claims process.
- If an insurance company denies or delays your claim, they must give you a reasonable explanation.

While many events are black-and-white concerning whether or not the policy should respond to a given claim, there are many gray areas where a company may elect to deny payment rather than pay a claim — because that decision is monetarily in their best interest. As stated earlier, in such situations, claims adjusters might question underwriters, or employees in the Policy Development Department that if the policy language is not *clearly* stated in the policy, the policyholder generally should prevail if the disagreement moves to the court system. Courts view the insurance contract as *strictly enforceable* because the insurance policy is a **unilateral** document (drafted by only one party — the insurance company) in which the policyholder has no input in the development of the contract (this is also known as a "contract of adhesion"). As a result, ambiguities are decided in favor of the insurance consumer. However, the problem ultimately becomes how long and how hard does a policyholder want to fight about coverage issues? Often, they give up too soon or forego use of an *attorney, consultant,* or a *public adjuster,* whereas the attorney, consultant or public adjuster may be able to resolve a claim in the policyholder's favor.

An example from my own insurance company experience will drive this point home. One of the companies I worked for (which is no longer in business) offered a coverage called "*voluntary property damage,*" which was often purchased by contractors (landscape gardeners, carpenters, plumbers, electricians, etc.). The intent of the coverage endorsement was to delete an exclusion in the general liability portion of the insurance policy that pertained to property in the policyholder's care, custody or control. For instance, if I am a painter and I go inside your house to paint a room, the entire room I will be painting is deemed to be in my care, custody or control. If I happen to poke a hole in the wall with my ladder, the hole in the wall is something that will **not** be covered by my insurance policy. The voluntary property damage endorsement was meant to provide coverage for this type of situation.

However, the way my prior employer worded the endorsement, intended coverages were not actually provided by the endorsement in a great number of care, custody or control claims situations. While there was not a huge premium charge for the endorsement, it was sold for many years without technically providing coverage for several claims related to care, custody or control — which, again, was why the endorsement was developed to begin with.

It would have been relatively easy to add additional coverage by clarification of policy language intent, but this was never done. Why not? Due to the small premium charge, it wasn't worth the insurance company's time and effort to correct the problem. It would have taken considerable time for the people from the Information Technology Department to re-program the computers, time for people from the Policy Development Department to recommend new wording, time to re-file the policy wording with the Department of Insurance, time to provide updates and training to the Underwriting and Claims Departments advising of the new wording, and so forth. Clearly, this decision was not in the best interest of the policyholder, but it was deemed a good business decision by insurance company management on a purely "cost of change" basis.

Consumers remain confused about the insurance claims process for many different reasons. One reason is that a claim involves understanding policy language and things such as coverage provisions, limitations and exclusions. Another reason for consumer confusion is a lack of information about the process itself — and due to a great amount of misinformation that has been spread by friends, relatives, neighbors and others concerning insurance claims.

Common types of property claims include hail, wind, lightning, water and theft. And, while not frequent, fire is still one of the most catastrophic types of property claims that occur.

Other events that may result in significant claims include personal liability claims, at-fault automobile accidents, on-premises medical injuries, and other types of situations where policyholders are deemed legally liable ("negligent") in some manner. It is interesting to note that according to industry statistics for homeowners insurance claims, property damage and theft claims account for nearly 80% of all claims payments, while liability claims account for less than 10% of claims paid by insurance companies.

Please understand that there are very few hard and fast rules in the area of claims. There are several reasons for this. First, each claim must *stand on its own merits*. The facts surrounding each claim are all-important. For example, consider a hail storm that occurs. Two next door neighbors turn claims in to their respective insurance companies. One day soon after, the two neighbors are talking and discover that one of them got a claim check from their insurer for $4,500 to replace his roof and the other received no payment at all. In the course of investigating the facts, it was discovered that the neighbor who received a claim payment had a 25-year-old roof, and the other had his roof replaced just last year. This single fact highlights a logical explanation for this claims handling discrepancy: old roofs are easily damaged, while new roofs are very resilient against hail. Thus, each of these two claims was handled properly.

Second, there is some *flexibility* among insurance companies in the area of underwriting. One company may file their automobile insurance program with a rule that "forgives" the policyholder's first automobile physical damage claim if the policyholder has been insured continuously for five or more years. Another company may not have filed this same rule and, instead, surcharges for any at-fault accident that exceeds a stated threshold dollar amount, such as $500.

Third, there are *gray areas* in the insurance policy. It is impossible for insurance policies to contemplate *every single claim situation* that might ever arise. Do you have a hard time believing this? As an expert witness in court for insurance-related cases, I assure you this is true. Courts are constantly addressing insurance policy coverage questions.

Some of the many questions that insurance consumers have concerning claims include:

- Will my policy be cancelled if I turn in a claim?
- Will my insurance rates increase if I make a claim?
- Am I better off paying small claims out-of-pocket, or should I turn in every possible claim to my insurance company?
- Are claims that I make under my business insurance policy viewed in the same way as claims I make under my personal insurance policies?
- What are my options if coverage for my claim is denied by my insurance company?

For the reasons previously outlined, keep in mind that there may be different outcomes in the way that adjusters will handle two similar claims. Nevertheless, here are reasonable answers to the above questions.

*Will my policy be cancelled if I turn in a claim?*

Maybe — depending on the type of claim, the number of claims you have made in a specific time period and the underwriting criteria in place at your insurance company. You can ask your insurance agent what impact making a claim will have, but know this: insurance agents are required to inform insurance companies about what you tell them. Therefore, it is possible that your situation may be held against you even if you do not turn in the claim. For example, if you purchased a dangerous breed of dog (e.g. a pit bull), did not inform your insurance company and the dog bit a neighbor's child.

While you may not realize it, insurers are interested in any significant changes that occur in the risks they are accepting. In insurance company terminology this is known as a "material change in risk." So, if you had no animals when you first purchased your homeowners policy, the insurance company expects that will remain the case throughout the time that they provide your insurance. But if you buy a dog, this presents a different set of circumstances from the standpoint that the dog could cause damage (destroy property) or injure someone (jump on them or bite them).

Generally, the owner of a dog is held liable for damages or injury the dog causes, and the specific breed mentioned above is more prone to cause injuries than other breeds. The worst scenarios involve children under seven years of age. When a child is younger than seven, courts may feel they have not reached the "age of reason," and since their judgment is not yet formed, they cannot be held liable for their actions — including things such as teasing a dog. If the child is not liable, *you* are. If you are liable for injuries, your insurance company may step in to pay damages you owe. If they didn't know you have a dog, they definitely will not look favorably upon paying a claim involving a dog.

*Will my insurance rates increase if I make a claim?*

In the past, homeowner policies did not necessarily go up. However, insurance company homeowner results have deteriorated significantly over the past few years due to factors such as natural catastrophes and more. Therefore, your homeowner policy may now very well cost you more if you make a claim against it. Concerning automobile policies, you are very likely to pay more (via a policy "surcharge") for any at-fault accident. In addition, your auto policy price will likely increase if a household driver receives a ticket for any type of moving violation. Statistically speaking, nearly 1/3 of fatal accidents involve speeding or driving too fast for conditions. If you speed, insurers have proven that any accident you have in the future will be more severe than if you do not speed. Therefore, you are charged a higher rate *now* for the accident that may occur in the *future.*

*Am I better off paying small claims out of pocket or turning in each claim?*

It may benefit you *not* to turn in small claims. It does, however, depend on on the type of claim and the facts involved. For instance, if $520 of personal clothing is stolen out of your car, and if you carry a $500 deductible, it makes little sense to turn in the claim. However, if someone slips and falls in front of your house on an icy sidewalk that you did not shovel for three days and is injured, you *should* turn in the claim, even if the injured person says that they will not hold you liable. This type of claim may worsen over time and turn ugly for a variety of reasons, so it is important to provide your insurance company with information concerning the situation as soon as possible, so they can investigate and hire defense counsel should the need arise. In fact, if you do not turn in this type of claim, the insurance company has the right to reject payment for this very reason. This is known as prejudicing the insurance company's rights by not giving them the opportunity to become involved at the time that the accident took place.

*Are claims I turn in under my business insurance policy viewed the same way as claims I make under my personal insurance policies?*

No, most business policies are underwritten on a "loss ratio" basis. This means that insurance company underwriters weigh the amount of premiums "paid in" against the amounts of claims dollars "paid out." While different companies apply different profitability criteria, most insurance companies are content with a pure loss ratio of 50% or less. However, the higher the loss ratio, the more likely that a higher renewal price increase will be applied.

Conversely, under homeowners and automobile policies, insurance companies typically take a long, hard look at the frequency of losses incurred. Since homeowners' premiums are generally less than $1,000 annually, insurance companies cannot afford to pay out many claims and hope to remain profitable. While automobile insurance rates are somewhat higher, payments for liability and medical claims can involve significant payments. Again, insurance companies cannot pay many high automobile claims for one policyholder and remain profitable. What about a policyholder who has several very small claims? Underwriters adhere to the following rule: *frequency breeds severity*. In other words, if a policyholder has a history of small claims, a big claim is almost certain to follow at some point in the future.

*What are my options if coverage for my claim is denied by my insurance company?*

A good first step is to discuss the situation with your insurance claims adjuster. Make certain they understand the facts clearly. If they have denied your claim they should cite the specific policy language upon which they rely. If you continue to feel the insurance company has wrongly denied your claim, you should next discuss your claim with your insurance agent. Your agent has a legal, dual fiduciary responsibility to act not only in the insurance company's best interest, but also in your best interest. Keep in mind, however, your agent likely has thousands or millions of dollars of written premiums with the insurance company compared to the couple of thousands of dollars that you pay for your insurance. Therefore, agents may have the inherent bias that works in the favor of the insurance company. After all, if they lose you as a client it may cost them $1,000 or so of insurance commission income, whereas if they lose their insurance company contract it may cost them $100,000 or more of income. Another factor may be that your insurance agent makes it a personal practice not to get involved with claims because of the feeling that adjusters are in the very best position to interpret claims.

After discussing your situation with your insurance adjuster and your insurance agent to no avail, you may next wish to discuss your claim denial with a public adjuster, an insurance consultant or an attorney. Also, you may wish to involve the Commissioner of Insurance in your applicable state where coverages apply (typically in your "state of domicile") by filing a complaint and asking that they review the circumstances of your claim denial.

Yes, it is possible that your insurance company made a mistake, or that your claim may involve a gray area under the insurance policy where the insurance company has taken the position that benefits them rather than you. However, it has been my experience that the vast majority of insurance claims are handled efficiently and correctly by insurance company adjusters. Therefore, if your insurance claim has been denied, it is quite possible that there truly is no coverage for your claim under your insurance policy.

Keep in mind that payment of claims is the reason insurance companies are in business. However, they must follow their policy (contract) wording during the claims adjustment process. If they pay claims that are not covered under the insurance policy then many other facets of the insurance coverage process are affected, such as:

- Policy rates will go up since actuaries did not contemplate payment for uncovered claims
- Courts may broaden the insurance company's liability for other claims that were never intended to be covered. This can result from a plaintiff's attorney asking the insurance company if they ever intentionally paid claims that were not covered by their insurance contract.
- Claims adjusters, underwriters and the Marketing Department may become confused concerning coverages provided under insurance policies sold to the public.

One final comment is warranted in the area of claims. Some insurance companies use only their own **inside** insurance adjusters; some insurance companies use mainly "independent contractor" (third-party, or **outside**) adjusters, and other insurance companies use a combination of inside and outside adjusters. As a general statement, I have found that third-party adjusters do not handle claims as well as adjusters who are insurance company employees. My guess is that this is due to several factors such as lack of training; frequency of employee turnover in independent adjuster companies; performance based upon a different "customer" base (for inside adjusters, their customer is their policyholder; for third-party adjusters, their customer is the insurance company itself). There may also be a possible lack of accountability, i.e., complaints against individual company adjusters go directly to insurance company claims supervisors; complaints against independent adjusters may never get back to appropriate insurance company personnel.

Are all third-party independent adjusters bad adjusters? Certainly not. However, during my career I have noticed that there generally is a difference between employee adjusters and third-party adjusters and that the balance tips in favor of inside adjusters doing a better job overall.

## Underwriting

*Underwriting* is the analysis of the characteristics of a risk to decide if the risk is *acceptable, unacceptable,* or *acceptable if certain requested conditions (changes) are met.* The underwriter reviews applications that are submitted and decides if the characteristics presented meet company guidelines that are in place for that particular type of business (such as homeowner, auto or business owner policies).

By its very nature, underwriting is discriminatory. Underwriters apply a set of criteria, and many times are also allowed personal leeway (known as "underwriting judgment") when making decisions on specific accounts.

The underwriter typically has the power to make exceptions to the insurance company's guidelines and to issue a policy based on a submission—even though that submission does not technically qualify. If an exception is made, it is typically documented, and is frequently reviewed by management.

Underwriters also possess **pricing** authority. This is true in both personal lines and commercial lines, though much more evident on large commercial accounts. The most frequent pricing structure used in personal lines (auto and homeowner policies) is application of *preferred credits,* or use of a *tiered* approach. Whichever method of pricing is used, the idea is that the best risks (those that the company underwriter feels will have no future claims) get the best pricing. This is not always the case, however, as favors are frequently done on the underwriting level based on things such as an underwriter's relationship with an agent.

One of the craziest things about the underwriting process is the archaic *rating methodology* that is used to price commercial lines (business insurance) policies. There is no good (quick and easy-to-use) rating system that is widely available in the insurance industry.

Some insurance companies have developed proprietary rating systems and do provide their field underwriters with the capability to price insurance products outside of the office. However, once the insurance products are quoted in the field, arcane rating systems are used back at the home office in order to get insurance policies issued.

A tremendous amount of effort and time is required to rate coverages that the insurance company provides. All the customer and agent want is a bottom line price. They don't care how difficult it is to massage the insurance company's computer software to come up with a price. Much of the problem has to do with the history of commercial lines ratemaking and the fact that "it has always been done this way." What is needed is a major overhaul of the commercial lines products rating methodologies in order to simplify the way that accounts are priced. The result will be a welcome reduction in the amount of time it takes to issue a commercial insurance policy, as well as a better understanding by consumers of how prices are determined (greater transparency).

## Policy Services

*Policy Services* provides the internal assistance necessary for the insurance company to get their policies issued. This includes rating entry, secretarial-related work, and other jobs that move a policy through the organization and out their doors.

Many insurance companies also include some type of *quality control* as part of their Policy Services Department. Quality control entails the review of issued policies to ascertain whether they contain the policy forms, endorsements, exclusions and other items that match the insurance coverage requested by the consumer.

Amazingly enough, some insurance companies have completely done away with the quality control function. For example, during a recent deposition I discovered that a large, national insurance company relies completely upon their insurance agents to review issued policies for accuracy. The attorney for the insurance carrier stated that the insurance company feels it is the responsibility of their insurance agent representatives to review policies as part of the services the agency provides to earn the commissions paid by the insurance company. I find this stance utterly amazing. This position is similar to the automobile manufacturer producing a new vehicle and expecting the dealership that sells the car to perform a product safety check of the car. To me, common sense dictates that the party that has the most knowledge about the product being produced should implement quality control procedures.

## Audit Department

The main purpose of the *Audit Department* is to find out if there have been changes in a commercial policy since the last anniversary date. Many commercial insurance policies are issued on an "auditable" basis. This means that the initial insurance premium is based upon an estimate — a best-guess as to what the business exposure will be at the end of the policy term. Auditable insurance policies include General Liability, Worker's Compensation, Business Automobile, and may include certain other policies such as Commercial Inland Marine and some Non-Standard insurance policies. Auditable policies are rated based upon estimated "exposures." For example, General Liability rating may be based upon things such as square footage (area), gross sales receipts, units, payroll, admissions, or "A-Rates" where underwriting judgment is used to determine a rate to charge for the exposure. For Worker's Compensation, rates are based upon worker job duties (classifications); and payrolls are assigned to each classification on the current policy.

Here is an example of an auditable policy situation: Acme Widgets has an insurance policy that is effective January 1, 2014, and expires on January 1, 2015. Acme plans sales of $1,000,000 during the 2014 policy year. Therefore, the insurance policy is issued using a specific rate (i.e., 1.57 per $1,000 of sales), which is chosen by the underwriter. This rate is then applied to the estimated sales value. The policy is issued with a General Liability premium of $1,570, which reflects the 1.57 rate x 1,000 exposure units ($1,000,000 dollars of sales). The policy is audited six months after the end of the policy term (June 30, 2015) and it is discovered that Acme actually sold $2,000,000 worth of widgets during the policy period.

In this case, an additional premium is developed taking the 1.57 specific rate and multiplying it by 1,000 additional sales exposure units (representing the additional $1,000,000 of sales that took place during 2011). Another $1,570 of premium is owed to the insurance company as a result of the **actual** sales that took place at Acme Widgets. This is fair to all parties because additional sales represent additional exposure to risk for the insurance company and they are entitled to additional premium to offset the additional risks present. Alternately, if only $500,000 in sales were generated by Acme during 2014, they would be entitled to a credit of $785 for the reduced exposure basis. If a credit is due to the policyholder, a check is issued by the insurance company and sent to the policyholder.

Note that there are some insurance policies that are issued on a non-auditable basis. Generally, this is a positive situation for the insurance customer because it allows businesses to better budget their annual insurance costs, and it can result in cost-savings for businesses that are growing. However, for those businesses with declining sales, an auditable policy is best since they will get money refunded when an audit takes place after the policy period ends.

## Loss Control

*Loss Control* (also known as *Loss Control Engineering* or *Safety Engineering*) is a service offered by insurance companies to clients who meet certain criteria. These criteria include the class of business (a manufacturing business certainly warrants loss control while a small ice cream store generally does not); premiums generated by the account (many insurance companies do not feel it is cost effective to offer these types of services to an account that generates less than $25,000, or so, of annual insurance premium); and on a case-by-case basis (usually as a result of customer or agent request).

Loss control is a valuable service if the individual performing the inspection is well-trained and experienced in looking at the particular type of business you own. Where this potential benefit fails is when the loss control inspector is not knowledgeable, or when business owners do not follow through on specific key recommendations generated during the personal inspection of their business.

Loss control can work miracles in bringing down both the frequency and severity of Worker's Compensation injuries. Loss control engineers can help implement safety programs, and they work with Human Resources, as well as supervisors and foremen, to ensure the success of safety programs. They also address things such as potential products liability claims and whether or not the business is complying with current work-related laws and regulations (i.e., OSHA). However, the most important thing that loss control engineers can do is to get owners or top-level managers involved in key loss control issues. If top management is not 100% behind recommended changes, necessary loss control changes—and resulting business improvements—will simply not occur.

Never underestimate the importance of good company management. I have worked with companies that have had a mentality of "good enough" or that were unwilling to instill sound operating practices because of the "hassle factors" involved with making changes. Insurance companies seldom desire to insure this type of company. On the other hand, I have seen a change of management come with a corresponding change of operational mentality. New management enacted new policies, procedures and safety requirements and the difference was amazing. Where old management was content with no changes, new management abhorred claims and became much more profitable as a result. The increased profitability resulted in part from reduced insurance premiums due to improved claims results. Same company name but a completely different management mindset.

For effective loss control, the insurance company representative should visit the business a minimum of twice per year. Four times to twelve times per year may be necessary initially. This would depend on the type of business, the focus of the loss control initiatives (i.e., Worker's Compensation vs. premises liability related) and/or the severity of problems that are discovered. But more than likely, the insurance company will not offer this frequency of visits, so it is up to the customer to demand it.

Alternative sources of information are available if your business does not meet the minimum qualifications for insurance company loss control services. These include hiring private loss control engineering firms, requesting an OSHA inspection, or using other state or local government agencies.

A business can request a free OSHA inspection to see if they are in compliance with federal laws. The OSHA inspector will point out areas of non-compliance (if any) and will not levy a fine for any deficient areas discovered during this process.

Other resources may be available, depending on the state in which your business is located. For example, in the State of Wisconsin, a Worker's Compensation classification code audit can be provided by an entity known as the Worker's Compensation Rating Bureau (WCRB). In the course of their inspection, they will also point out safety concerns that they might observe.

# 3

## Other Insurance Company Support Positions

There are other positions at insurance companies that operate behind the scene and can impact how you are treated as an insurance company policyholder. These positions support the infrastructure of insurance companies and can include *Legal, Actuary, Subrogation, Internal Audit, Product Development, Information Technology* and *Management.*

### Legal

The *Legal Department* supports the Claims Department. It ultimately decides which claims should be fought (company position defended), which "outside" attorneys (independent, stand-alone law firms that represent insurance companies and their insureds) will be used in litigation support matters, and at what point a settlement should be considered. In my experience, most "internal" attorneys do not possess the same depth of legal courtroom expertise as those attorneys who practice law as a part of a law firm. Thus, outside attorneys usually represent the concerns of the insurance company in court.

Company attorneys may also provide support to Human Resources and other internal departments concerning setting of guidelines and policies, as well as providing guidance on internal claims and suits, such as Worker's Compensation claims and employment-related practices suits for things such as age discrimination. An ancillary reason that outside attorneys are used by insurance companies is to avoid possible conflict of interest claims by their insureds. If an insurance company uses its own attorneys to represent its insureds, it may be accused of acting in its own best interest—i.e., by trying to pay as little as possible for a claim, regardless of the merits.

An example of this would be a situation where an insurance company's insured was sued as the result of negligent operation of a motor vehicle. If the injuries are substantial and the policy liability limits are low, the insurance company may not even want to spend money on defense of their insured. However, this exposes the policyholder's personal assets. Courts have decided that the duty to defend is as important, if not more important, than the duty to pay for damages. Insurance companies may be able to "pay and walk," but must be very careful in these situations.

Another reason outside law firms are used is because of the wide variety of subject matter expertise offered by external law firms. It is difficult for lawyers to be experts in all areas of law, thus, if expertise is required in special areas such as products liability, product recall, pollution, etc., attorneys are sought out who possess this specific expertise. Also, external attorneys have more experience in preparing for and presenting the insurance company's position before a judge should the case move to trial.

## Actuary

"Kill the actuaries" is the battle-cry of many underwriters and marketing representatives. The purpose of those in the *Actuarial Department* is to statistically analyze the rate structure of insurance policies by line of business (i.e., commercial property, commercial general liability, commercial automobile, homeowners and personal automobile) to decide whether a rate increase or decrease is needed, and if so, by how much.

Ratemaking is often a matter of massaging the numbers to say what you want them to say. For example, actuarial data for an insurance company's State of Wisconsin homeowners policies (referred to as "book of business") may call for an overall increase of 10% based upon statistics gathered by their Actuarial Department. This rate increase may be based on a review of the company's income and expenses, where total premiums (income) received is compared to the company's expenses. Insurance company expenses include claims paid, outstanding liabilities (known as "incurred but not reported" or "IBNR" within the industry) and other company expenses such as payroll, benefits, overhead and profit.

This 10% rate increase recommended by Actuarial is then reviewed by Marketing and/or Underwriting (depending on where the responsibility for this task falls). Joint discussions are then held between these departments and senior management to determine the ultimate policy price increase that will be taken. Discussions may include areas such as statutory rate adequacy, marketing competitiveness, and future income and expense projections (including regulatory impact, time value of money, and so on).

Rate discussions are always a balancing act. The insurance company must charge enough money to stay solvent but cannot charge too much compared to its competition. If pricing gets too far above competitor pricing, the insurance company is likely to not only shut down new business income, but may also lose existing business on the books. The result is that profitability will suffer. An additional factor that insurance companies must keep in mind is that their best customers may leave (i.e., automobile policyholders with good credit ratings, good driving records and claims-free) if prices are raised too much. The customers who are left will be less profitable, which further deteriorates the insurance company's bottom-line.

My experience is that a great deal of emphasis is placed upon marketing competitiveness during actuarial discussions. The Marketing Department often plays a lead role in discussions and is typically successful in convincing senior management that, although actuarial data may call for a 10% statewide increase, a lower percentage of increase should be implemented due to marketplace competitiveness.

Understand that the above example is quite simplified. In reality, much fine-tuning takes place during the ratemaking process. For instance, rates in one territory with poor experience may be supported (off-set) by another territory with good experience.

This means that, rather than taking a 10% statewide homeowners rate increase, insurance companies segment rate information using a multitude of factors. Using homeowners as an example, some of the factors considered include the age of the home, its value, the geographical territory, liability values, protection class and much more. As a result of this ratemaking process, the insurance company's homeowner rates may ultimately decrease for homes located in Milwaukee, Wisconsin, but this will be offset by taking a 20% increase for homes insured in Superior, Wisconsin. Therefore, the desired net effect of a 10% overall increase for the insurance company as a whole is achieved.

Once new rates are agreed upon, the company files its rates with the Department of Insurance in the state(s) where the new rates will be in effect. Where a **file-and-use** law is in effect, the insurance company must submit its new rates before they become effective. Actual approval is *not* required before the rates are used. However, the Department of Insurance can disapprove the rates if they find them in violation of any statutes. To play it safe, insurers often wait until after the Department of Insurance has reviewed and approved their rates just to make sure that their company will not need to re-call their new rates after they have been published and distributed to their agency sales force.

If a **prior-approval** law is in effect, all rates must be filed with the state's Department of Insurance (Insurance Commissioner's office) prior to use and must be *formally* approved or disapproved.

It cannot be over-emphasized that the setting of rates presents a difficult dichotomy for insurance companies. Regardless of what the mathematical models may say, the insurance company must compete in the real world against other companies trying to sell similar products. If an actuary suggests a rate increase of 20% and this puts the insurance company's pricing structure at a total of 15% over marketplace competitors, very little additional new business is likely to be written. On the other hand, by completely ignoring the actuary's findings, the company is jeopardizing its surplus (the funds available for paying future claims).

## Subrogation

*Subrogation Department* personnel are known as the "bad boys" of the insurance company. They typically work as a part of the Claims Department and chase down individuals or companies that owe money to the insurance company. If, for instance, an automobile accident occurs where someone other than you (the policyholder) is clearly at fault in damaging your car, or injuring you or other occupants in your car, your insurance company may *directly* pay you for damages, bodily injuries or medical payments.

However, your insurance company is then entitled to subrogate against the at-fault party. Since the legal system holds individuals responsible for damages that result from their negligence, the at-fault party must pay to make the innocent party whole. When your insurance company makes payment to you, they are then entitled to "step into your shoes" to recover payments from the negligent party who was responsible for your accident.

The first step in the subrogation process is to determine whether or not the at-fault party has insurance. While there are still many people who do not purchase insurance, the vast majority do carry insurance. The easiest way to determine whether an insurance policy is in effect is to send a letter directly to the person who caused the accident. The letter states that they are personally responsible for all damages to innocent parties; however, if they provide their insurance company information, their insurance company will be dealt with directly.

As someone who has had responsibility for subrogation earlier in my insurance career, I can attest that people are generally unco-operative when it comes to admitting their fault and in sharing their insurance company information. It is not at all uncommon to send three or more requests for information.

If the negligent party does not have insurance, he or she will per-sonally owe the amount of damages for the repair of the policyhold-er's banged-up vehicle, as well as medical payments, etc., and must ultimately pay any outstanding legal judgment on an out-of-pocket basis. Payment plans, including garnishment of wages, may be set up for repayment of what is owed.

More and more insurance companies are turning their attention to subrogation. Why is this? Because of the potential to recoup dol-lars paid out to policyholders. Some subrogation efforts amount to thousands or even hundreds of thousands of dollars. However, even small dollar amounts can add up to significant dollar amounts for insurance companies.

In addition, insurance companies are becoming more aggres-sive in pursuing certain specific types of subrogation. For instance, companies are recognizing the potential that Worker's Compensa-tion subrogation holds. Insurance companies must pay Work Comp claims according to state statutes that generally demand payment on a "no fault" basis. In other words, if an employee is injured due to a work-related occurrence, insurance companies must make payment to the employee for the incurred injury. However, it is possible that the injury was the result of the negligence of a third party (unrelated to the employer). In this situation, the insurance company is enti-tled to demand payment from the at-fault third party. If the negli-gent party does not agree to make payment based upon the demand letter, the insurance company that made payment is legally entitled to bring a lawsuit against the negligent party.

Many times, outside collection agencies or attorneys are used for subrogation purposes where the potential of a large dollar recovery amount exists. Understand that these people can play hardball! In some of these types of outsourced subrogation situations, the subrogation firms are paid based upon a percentage of the total dollar recovery amount. As a result, they are aggressive not only in their attempts to receive payment, but also related to the dollar amounts sought.

## Internal Audit

The *Internal Audit* Department reviews internal insurance company underwriting, claims, and other Department activities to make sure the various Departments within the insurance company are acting within company guidelines. Many times management requests that a certain underwriting line of business, or a particular type of claim adjuster file (i.e., liability adjuster), be reviewed to see if there are possible areas for improvement. Another reason for internal review of underwriting and claims files is to discover whether any wrongdoing (i.e., fraud) has occurred. Auditors look for both isolated situations as well as patterns of negative activities that have occurred. Auditors review files, note observations and make recommendations for change in the hopes of seeing improvements in the near future.

Internal audit also monitors things such as possible vendor (or agent, etc.) kickbacks to employees or expense report accuracy, and they ascertain whether employees are doing their jobs honestly. I have known of situations where claims adjusters invented a "dummy" corporation and then began making claims payments to their dummy corporation for building repairs—while in reality pocketing all of the money.

I have also seen situations where agents take money from clients but keep the money and pay their clients' claims out of their own private bank accounts. Here, insurance policies were *never actually issued* and the insurance company was unaware that the person had purchased insurance. Never heard of such a thing? Insurance companies rarely, if ever, report this type of fraud since it gives them very bad press and makes their other policyholders nervous.

## Product Development

Insurance companies are a strange lot. They tout their differences and state reasons why they are better than their competitors. However, many times, companies sell very similar products at similar prices whether they are selling homeowners, automobile or businessowners policies. One of the reasons for this is that insurance companies often use the same rates and coverage language as their basis of coverage—items that are provided by the Insurance Services Office (ISO) or the American Association of Insurance Services (AAIS). Since the insurance policy is a contract, insurers are comfortable using contract language that has been "court tested." While prior lawsuits provide valuable case law for insurance carriers, it also ties their hands when it comes to offering innovative products in the marketplace. The result is that many insurance companies sell nearly identical "black boxes."

While customers might want a black-and-white box, the company says all it can offer is a black box, take it or leave it. Often times, the customer is either left unsatisfied, or continues to look for alternate ways to get what they want from an insurance coverage standpoint.

Most companies keep pretty close tabs on what their competitors are up to. If a new product is introduced by the competition, other companies typically wait for six months or so to see how well the product has been received in the marketplace. If the new product has generated decent revenues, while incurring limited claims payments, other companies in essence copy the new product that the trend-setting company introduced.

Everyone at insurance companies keeps their eyes and ears open concerning their competition, but typically it is the Marketing Department that feeds competitive information back to their insurance company management. Once the information is received, the Marketing Department makes suggestions for change, if they feel it makes sense. Senior management from both Claims and Underwriting then either agree or disagree with the recommendation(s). If consensus is reached within the insurance company departments, the product idea moves forward through the *Product Development* team, and a new product is born. The proposed product is then reviewed by other departments, such as the Legal and Information Technology Departments, prior to release.

Since some of the items developed are new to a company, there may be some ambiguity concerning exactly what coverages are intended to be provided. As a result, there can be a period of time after a new product's introduction when the Claims Department has internal discussions concerning whether or not certain claims that have been made should or should not be paid by the insurance company.

## Information Technology

Programming of new products by the Information Technology Department (IT) is an extremely important part of the introduction of new insurance company products. In fact, this single department can cause a new product to be put on hold for a short time, or even indefinitely. Therefore, insurance companies often start the new product development process by having discussions with the Information Technology Department to make certain that they have the capacity to provide programming support for the introduction of the new product.

Keep in mind that insurance policies are basically issued as the result of software programming. Policy language, attachments (known as "endorsements") and rating to achieve a price all result from software programming. Some insurance companies develop all of their own forms, which requires a large investment in IT programming dollars. Other companies purchase parts of their policy formatting or rating programs from third parties. But no matter what approach is taken by insurance companies, the Information Technology Department plays a key role in their organization. There is always some kind of work for them to do.

The Information Technology Department at insurance companies operates in much the same way as the assembly line at a car manufacturer. This is the "guts" of the production process and this is the department that can bottleneck the entire insurance company organization. There are many more projects on the table than there are people to program requested changes. Time constraints, as well as computer system constraints, play important roles in what can be offered by insurance companies. In addition, insurance products themselves are much more systems-dependent than many other types of business products.

An example of one major project addressed by insurance companies was the "Year 2000" (Y2K) issue. It was a massive undertaking by insurance companies because it affected nearly every facet of their business—policy wording, agency contracts, suppliers and vendors, as well as simply requiring that insurance companies made certain that their future policies were issued with the correct dates.

In addition to providing programming for new products, the Information Technology Department is charged with maintenance of existing computer systems. This includes updating the software programs, addressing problems that pop up at individual workstations and solving a multitude of other technological issues as they arise.

## Management

It is impossible to talk about an insurance company without mentioning its *Management*. Companies are driven by the departments previously discussed. Some companies' top management focus on claims, some on sales and some on underwriting. As a very general statement, many of the direct writer insurance company top management focus on underwriting, while companies that sell through independent agencies tend to focus on sales.

Some decisions faced by insurance company management involve federal and state legislation. At times insurance companies attempt to impact *future* legislation in such ways as having lobbyists express their opinions to lawmakers. However, most of the time insurance companies *react* to legislation that has been passed. Insurance is a heavily regulated industry because it deals with the "public good." As a result, laws pertaining to insurance change frequently.

An example is **Proposition 103**, which passed in California several years ago. This law mandated insurance price rollbacks.

Other examples include the **Terrorism Risk Insurance Act** (TRIA), first passed in November, 2002, and reauthorized under the Terrorism Risk Insurance Extension Act (TRIEA) in 2005 and again in 2007 with the Terrorism Risk Insurance Program Reauthorization Act (TRIPRA), which extended TRIP through December 31, 2014. These laws require that the federal government act as a backstop in situations involving severe damage resulting from terrorist attacks.

Indeed, legislation has a huge impact on the insurance industry. In addition, the trend has been for regulatory bodies that are responsible for oversight of the insurance sector to become more and more liberal (pro-consumer) in their approach to dealing with conflicts that arise between insurance companies and consumers.

There are other factors that are beyond an insurance company's control but can have a tremendous effect on its future profitability. New competitors can enter a particular geographic area or introduce a new or enhanced insurance product into the marketplace with very aggressive pricing. Existing carriers may need to match that pricing or risk losing market share. Unexpected catastrophes can strike several different times during a single year. Tornadoes, hail storms, hurricanes, terrorism, as well as large losses can deplete a company's surplus.

Large losses are defined differently by each insurance company. For some, it may be a claim that exceeds $10,000 paid out. For another insurance company, it may be defined as losses that exceed $100,000. Rest assured, however, that any loss that reaches the limit of insurance stated on the policy declarations page (generally the first page of your insurance policy—where a summary of limits and coverages are shown) is considered a large loss. When a loss exceeds the limit of a primary insurance policy (the policy that pays first), the insurance company may be required to pay even more if an umbrella policy exists.

So, keeping these factors in mind, I have a question. Why do a great number of insurance companies obsess over strategic planning as far as five to ten or more years into the future? I have yet to figure that out.

Of course it makes sense to develop action plans to address things that are currently happening or things that might happen up to two years or so in the future. Included in this planning process timeline should be things such as the possibility of entering additional states, business product re-focus and the prices (rates) that will be charged for products. However, my experience has been that insurance company management often spend an inordinate amount of time trying to guess what will happen in the general marketplace, what will happen to the overall economy, future government regulation and all kinds of other things when there is no way to accurately predict the outcomes. Seldom does anyone correctly guess what the future holds for insurance—or for anything else.

How many people called the late-2008 ultra-bear market and the corresponding vast economic meltdown and economic recession? Did anyone foresee the terrorist attacks of September 11th that forever changed so many things in the United States? My point is that you might be lucky enough to have a good guess once or twice, but that's all it is— a guess. Yet, there exist some strategists who are so foolish that they actually believe they can determine and plan accordingly for the long-term impact that certain future occurrences might have on the insurance industry. Please give me a break! Better yet, insurance company management should give insurance customers a break and do something more worthwhile to earn their salaries.

One area of management decision-making that I find particularly disturbing concerns the best way to run insurance company operations. Some companies feel it is best to centralize operations. This means that most of the work (claims, policy issuance and underwriting) will be done out of one centrally located building. A year or so later, these same managers, or perhaps different managers who might currently be running the same company, then decide that it would be best to de-centralize their company operations by having multiple operating locations. Back and forth it goes with no ultimate cost savings realized on the insurance company's bottom line.

Another area that is constantly changing is how work is done within the confines of the insurance company. An insurance company may choose to have very linear, defined departments. An example of this is a company that has only underwriters in one department, claims adjusters in another department, marketing people in another department, etc. This same company may later decide that it would be good to have teams comprising underwriters, claims personnel, and marketing representatives sitting close to each other and interacting frequently. Management might then decide to go back to their original internal structure, or some combination of the two.

Please don't get me wrong. I believe that change can be good—especially at stodgy, conservative insurance companies. However, I have seen too many first-hand examples of significant change predicated upon non-logical, emotionally-based decisions. For instance, a national insurance company opened a large regional office simply because the senior vice-president they had hired to lead the office wanted to be located in a specific city and state.

Round-and-round it goes, where it stops nobody in insurance senior management positions seems to know. Inordinate amounts of money are spent changing where business is done and how it is done.

In some ways, it appears that the more something costs, the less attention it attracts. For example, an insurance company I previously worked for changed our company name only to later find out that it was too similar to the way another insurance company spelled their name. We were subsequently sued to cease and desist using our new name. Everything that contained our new name had to be changed. Think about the time and dollars involved, from re-programming to changing contracts and letterhead and so much more. To this day, I wonder about the ultimate cost of this major faux pas. I know that mistakes happen. However, how many senior managers, attorneys and others were involved with this decision? It would seem that someone along the way might have raised a red flag before final approval was made.

Another thing that insurance company management is sometimes guilty of is focusing on small, somewhat insignificant matters while losing sight of the big picture. For instance, supervisory level (and lower) might be instructed to make every attempt to keep expenses down. An example would be to avoid spending more than $50 per night at a hotel, or to make certain that all travel involving the purchase of airline tickets be scheduled two weeks or more in advance to save on the cost of plane tickets. This certainly makes sense. However, senior management at the same company may have no such constraints and are free to purchase airline tickets on a whim within 24 hours of the date of travel. This one occurrence negates the savings of several tickets purchased two weeks in advance. I understand that rank has its privilege to some extent. However, the bottom line is the bottom line. Management should not be above contributing to the financial success of the company.

## Reinsurance

Treaty          Facultative

# 4

## A Little Known Factor Affecting Insurance Companies

Most people don't realize the many different areas that impact their insurance policies. One such area is reinsurance. How does reinsurance affect the individual or the business that buys insurance? It impacts the amount of money you pay for your insurance policy. Let's find out how.

### Reinsurance

*Reinsurers* insure the insurance company. The term reinsurer came about from the concept of "re" being defined as "once again" as in to re-apply a coat of paint. Reinsurers pay for losses that occur under the specific contract that is signed between themselves and the insurance companies that they reinsure. Usually, these agreements provide reimbursement for catastrophic types of losses. Examples of catastrophes that may be reinsured range from wide-spread losses that occur over a large geographical territory (such as storm damages from hurricanes and tornadoes) to claims involving significant dollar amounts at a specific location (such as damages associated with the September 11, 2001 terrorist actions in New York.)

Reinsurance protects insurance companies from paying out a significant amount of their policyholder surplus (savings) in cases where the insurance company is obligated to pay out very large dollar amounts usually within a very short period of time. In these situations, reinsurers reimburse companies for amounts paid out. However, reinsurance is, in some ways, nothing more than a loan to the insurance company. When reinsurers make payments to insurance companies, they will often recoup their payout in the form of higher prices in future years for the reinsurance they provided to such insurance companies. This approach is similar to what happens with your policy when the primary insurance company increases its prices when you make claims under the policy.

Insurance companies typically purchase reinsurance in one of the following methods: *treaty*, *facultative* or *bordereau*. Companies can use all of these methods at the same time. **Treaty reinsurance** is negotiated across the insurance company's entire *book of business* according to agreed-upon criteria. For example, the criterion might be losses that fall within a dollar value range between $500,000 and $1,000,000. Treaties include many exclusions. One such exclusion may prohibit the insurance company from binding any business that fills propane tanks from the potential of a large loss due to explosion.

Treaty exclusions can be overcome when the reinsurer grants an "exception" or "accommodation." Sometimes these terms are used interchangeably. Other times, "exception" refers to a "minor" allowance of something excluded by the reinsurer, while "accommodation" refers to a "major" allowance. Using my propane tank example, the reinsurer will ask several specific, detailed questions and may agree to make an accommodation based upon answers given pertaining to the specific risk characteristics. One of the most important things that a business can do if it fills propane tanks is to make certain that their refill tank is located a significant distance (i.e., 100 feet or more) from any other combustible materials—buildings, contents, vehicles, etc. If not, the reinsurer will not make an accommodation.

One ancillary benefit of working with reinsurance companies is the opportunity for insurance company underwriters to gain additional knowledge about the kinds of risks involved in their various policies offered. Reinsurance underwriters are experts in their given area and freely share their knowledge with the insurance company underwriters that they work with.

**Facultative reinsurance** is purchased on a case-by-case basis when a specific risk falls outside of values that are contained within the treaty reinsurance agreement. An example is insuring a building valued at $1,500,000. Here, if treaty insurance allows values of up to $1,000,000 to be insured, facultative reinsurance would be purchased in the amount of $500,000.

When facultative reinsurance is purchased, an additional premium must be paid to the reinsurer to cover the additional exposure they have agreed to reinsure. While the purchase of facultative reinsurance was cumbersome in the past, today it is an easy process. Underwriters simply click on an icon on their computer, answer a few questions and a price for the cost of reinsurance comes back almost immediately. The reinsurance may be immediately bound and used to place the risk with the insurance company.

**Bordereau reinsurance** is purchased when an insurance company wishes to reinsure a specific set of risks. An example of this type of reinsurance is when a *book of business* is purchased from another insurance carrier and the purchasing company wishes to limit its loss exposures associated with the new book of business by purchasing reinsurance. A book of business refers to the purchase of several insurance policies from another insurance company. Book of business can be defined in a variety of ways, but examples could include one insurance company buying all personal automobile policies or all farm policies from another insurance company.

Make no mistake—you pay for reinsurance. With treaty reinsurance, it is a cost that is built into all insurance policies. With facultative reinsurance, an additional surcharge is added specifically to your insurance policy based upon your individual risk characteristics.

As reinsurance premiums to insurance companies increase, these costs are passed along to consumers in the way of policy premium increases. With the exception of the years 2001, 2002 and 2003, we have been in a "soft" underwriting cycle for the years 2000-2011. A soft cycle is defined as a time when consumer insurance premiums have remained mostly flat (unchanged), or may have even decreased somewhat. Part of the cause of this phenomenon has been due to reinsurance premiums staying relatively stable overall as the result of reinsurance company profitability.

In 2012 and 2013 the soft market began to "firm" (also referred to as a "hardening" of the insurance market) and the price that primary insurers began charging their policyholders began to rise, generally across all types of policies. The cost for many insurance policies rose by single digits, but it was not unusual to see price increases of 20% and higher.

The 2012-2013 market hardening also impacted the reinsurance companies. They began increasing their prices to insurance companies and this price was passed along by the primary insurers to their policyholders. If you go back to **Inside the Insurance Industry– Second Edition, ©2011** you will find that I correctly predicted when the current hardening of the insurance market would take place.

My current prediction is that the hardening market is here to stay for a few years. In most cases, single digit increases will be borne by policyholders, but insurers will not be reluctant to increase prices considerably for those accounts where loss experience has been poor. On the other hand, if you pay significant insurance premiums (the definition of significant varies from insurer to insurer) and have had good loss history (i.e., no losses for several years), you will be able to keep your pricing level or even reduce your cost of insurance in coming years. Although to reduce your pricing, you must obtain competitive quotes from insurance companies that do not currently provide your coverage.

# 5

## Pricing

One of the basic premises behind insurance is the **Law of Large Numbers**. This holds that "as more exposure units join the statistical group, losses become more predictable." In other words, insurance companies attempt to spread the losses of a few among the many who pay insurance premiums.

I had a recent conversation with my own insurance agent concerning a dramatic 35% increase in my homeowner policy price. He said that the insurer had experienced several catastrophic losses during the year and that they needed to increase prices in order to stay solvent. This is the *Law of Large Numbers* at work.

Insurance companies attempt to write policies insuring risk exposures that will not have losses, hoping to earn an underwriting profit. An underwriting profit occurs when premiums paid into the insurance company total more than the losses paid out by the insurance company, plus expenses incurred. It does *not* include other sources of income, such as investment income.

Here's the rub. The typical insurance consumer doesn't know whether he or she is adequately covered or whether they are paying a *fair price* in the marketplace for what they have purchased. They rely almost exclusively on what their insurance agent or insurance company tells them. That can be a big mistake!

Insurance companies tell agencies that represent them, and management at these insurance agencies pass along to their sales force the message that no one should "leave money on the table." This means insurance agents should try to sell insurance policies at the highest possible price while still closing the deal. In **personal lines** (automobile and homeowners) there are typically pricing "tiers" that customers may qualify for. These are controlled by underwriting guidelines, for the most part, but exceptions can be made to give customers a better deal than they would normally qualify for. Equate this to paying the sticker price for an automobile rather than obtaining a discount for the car you purchase. Most consumers have no idea that they may be able to qualify for a better price with the same company. Remember, it is in the insurance company's best interest to charge the highest possible price for their products since this helps improve their bottom line.

In **commercial lines** (businessowners, commercial property and general liability coverage) there is even more rate (price) flexibility. Technically, underwriters are charged with looking at the characteristics of a particular business and applying "credits" or "debits" to the particular business. However, policy pricing can depend upon non-risk characteristics. One such non-risk characteristic is the market cycle. In soft markets, most policies have some type of credit, and much pure underwriting credibility is lost. Credits tend to be applied haphazardly with little regard to the actual risk characteristics of a business. Instead, bottom line pricing rules.

In hard markets, the pendulum swings the other way and consumers are often charged more than their individual risk characteristics merit. As mentioned in the last chapter, this may be due to the increased price of reinsurance, or perhaps due to the fact that the insurance company previously had a bad year (for example, their combined ratio, defined as the ratio of income to expenses, was over 100%).

Sometimes, pricing a new business account amounts to nothing more than an underwriter asking their agent (or the client directly) how much the client is currently paying with their incumbent company—and then releasing a quote at a slightly lower price. The lower price is typically low enough to entice the prospective customer to move their insurance, but generally is not as low as the company could go.

There are special tools available to underwriters when they price accounts. *Experience rating* allows certain lines of commercial business to be further discounted, depending on an individual account's past loss history.

*A-rates* are judgment rates applied to certain general liability codes which allow the underwriter to price this line of business however they wish (using their best judgment). For instance, if I want to insure 1,000 acres of real estate development property (land), the judgment rate could be anywhere from .01 per acre to $100 or more per acre.

*Loss costs* are additional rating factors that are used by underwriters during the premium rating process. Loss costs are typically applied to commercial business policies and reflect the insurance company's profitability on certain segments within a line of business. For instance, loss costs can be applied separately to commercial automobile liability, automobile comprehensive, automobile collision, and other factors that make up the total premium for commercial automobile insurance. Generally, insurance companies are able to apply additional credits through the use of loss costs. However, if debits result from loss costs the resulting price may be adverse, thereby becoming uncompetitive.

General liability rates are usually based on sales (receipts), units, acres, or such similar measurement. General liability rates are filed with state Departments of Insurance based on "class codes," which differ according to the type of business being insured. As an example, a frozen food distributor has a class code of 13049, while a restaurant with no sales of alcoholic beverages—without a dance floor—a code 16814. Different types of businesses have different corresponding base rates.

Property rates are usually developed from Insurance Services Office (ISO) inspections. ISO physically inspects properties and provides insurance rates for insurance company use. These rates are based upon factors such as the building construction (i.e., frame, masonry, non-combustible), and fire protection (i.e., less than five road miles from the responding fire department or more than five road miles from the responding fire department). The developed rates are then accessed by insurance company underwriters who make an educated guess as to the probability that this particular property will be a good risk for the insurance company to insure.

The higher the probability of loss (i.e., a wooden building located fifteen miles from a responding fire department), the more premium on a "rate per $100 of value" basis the business or homeowner will pay. Alternately, the better the risk from a fire protection standpoint, the lower the rate per $100 that will be charged, such as when a business building has a masonry exterior and is located two blocks away from the responding fire department.

Commercial Automobiles are priced based on the *type* of vehicle (i.e., "heavy"—over 20,000 pounds), the *radius of operation* (i.e., "intermediate"—51 to 200 miles), whether or not there is a *fleet* (5 or more units), and business *usage* ("service" vs. "commercial" use). In addition, underwriters look at motor vehicle records of all persons who will be driving vehicles for the business. Again, the application of "credits," pricing tools such as experience rating, loss costs and IRPM (internal rate premium modification), can be applied to reduce the "manual" rate developed. Underwriters use their judgment when applying IRPM. Some insurance companies have internal guidelines concerning when, and how much, IRPM can be applied.

However, in nearly all cases, exceptions can be given by management to bring pricing down even further through the application of higher credit percentages.

Many Worker's Compensation policies offer dividends as an incentive for a business owner to write his work comp with a particular insurance carrier. While dividends are not guaranteed, they have a strong history of being paid on a regular basis. In addition to offering various dividend plans, some states allow companies to discount their rates through use of IRPM credits.

While covering the area of pricing it is important for you to understand that there are factors that can impact your personal or business insurance pricing that are beyond your control. One such factor is the decision by either insurance companies or insurance agencies, or both, to respond to their policyholders based on certain characteristics that you cannot change. For instance, an insurance company may decide that it no longer is interested in providing insurance coverage for a certain type of business—I'll use restaurants as an example.

Perhaps because a senior manager who is new to the insurance company has had a bad experience with restaurants at a previous employer, he decides that it is no longer in the best interest of his current insurance company employer to insure restaurants. As a result, an edict is sent to all underwriting staff to begin to "run off" restaurants that the company insures. This can be done in different ways, but usually involves applying significant price increases at renewal. Nothing about the restaurant has changed; its only sin is that it is no longer considered desirable from the insurance company's viewpoint. Eventually, the insurance company's restaurant policies may be sold to another insurance company that does not harbor similar negative feelings about restaurants.

A similar circumstance can take place at an insurance agency where through no fault of your own you begin to be treated differently. For example, an insurance agency may want to improve their profitability so they hire a 3rd party strategist (consultant). One of the consultant's suggestions may be for the agency to begin segmenting their business by premium volume (or commissions earned). One school of thought holds that insurance agencies need to spend more time with accounts that pay higher premiums and that the smaller accounts are a distraction. Therefore, the agency picks a number, say accounts that generate above $25,000 annual premium for commercial lines of business. Accounts that generate less are handled strictly by customer service representatives and are given no accommodations. The idea is to give them the very least amount of time possible and if the customer happens to leave, that is perfectly okay with the insurance agency.

As a business strategy, the insurance company and insurance agency's actions cannot be faulted. They are entitled to run their businesses the way that they desire. My issue with this type of insurance company and agency actions is that they seldom tell their customers about the new strategy. Therefore, if you do not pay attention to how you are treated by your insurance company and/or insurance agent, significant changes may be taking place that can cost you money.

As an insurance consumer, it is in your best interest to stay alert, notice when significant changes are made to your insurance coverages and/or pricing, and to ask questions. Things change over time and purchasers of insurance become complacent and wrongly have the opinion that their insurance company and insurance agent always have their best interests at heart.

If you find that your business is no longer welcome at your insurance company or agency, shop around. You are likely to find another insurer and agent who will happily provide insurance to you.

One last thing before we leave the topic of pricing. Return to the example of the automobile industry and how cars are sold. Manufacturers need to obtain a bottom-line price on models they sell in order to cover their expenses and to remain a going concern. Similarly, dealerships need a certain amount of profit (typically a percentage of gross revenues) to keep the doors open. However, the sale price varies from vehicle to vehicle, even for the same model. There are still people who pay sticker price for their cars and there are people who are ferocious negotiators. In the end, dealers net out all sales for their bottom line. Some pay more, some pay less, and the dealership makes enough money to cover their expenses and margin of profit.

It is much the same for insurance companies and insurance agencies. Some people accept whatever pricing their insurance company and insurance agent deliver, while others negotiate every single insurance policy premium. Overall, both the insurance company and insurance agency make enough money to stay in business even though prices paid may differ from customer to customer.

# 6

## External (Third Party) Resources

Insurance companies and insurance agencies employ several people to help them meet their business directives and to achieve their ultimate goal of profitability. But who works solely in the best interest of the insurance purchaser? Here are a couple of resources that do *not* contract with insurance carriers or agencies.

### Public Adjusters

Public adjusters are claims adjusters who work directly with businesses and individuals rather than for insurance companies. Generally, public adjusters are hired in the following circumstances:

- When a significant claim occurs for which the insurance company pays less than the policyholder feels is due under the policy (policy limit issues)
- When the insurance company tells its policyholder that they will not pay for a loss that the policyholder feels should be covered (coverage issues)

- To facilitate ease of presenting a claim to the insurance company after a large and complicated loss occurs—such as a major fire— (coverage expertise and time saving issues)

Public adjusters are consumer advocates who intercede on behalf of the policyholder with their insurance company. Public adjusters are paid directly by the policyholder and must be specifically licensed in many states.

There are not a great number of public adjusters in business across the United States. As a result, it is not uncommon for these individuals to travel across the entire country to provide services.

## Insurance Consultants

Insurance consultants provide professional insurance and risk management advice and services to clients, typically on a fee-only basis. One way to look at this profession is that they *provide insurance agent performance appraisals to businesses and individuals.*

Think about it. Company employees receive annual appraisals to let them know how they are performing in their job. Good employees are patted on the back, but since no one is perfect, there are also areas of improvement that are mentioned in their performance review. Employees who are not meeting expectations may be put on a formal action plan and may ultimately be let go.

How does a business or individual know whether their insurance agent is doing a good job if a performance appraisal is never completed? Oh sure, there are plenty of informal and emotionally-based performance reviews that are done. But mostly, if an insurance agent remembers your birthday, takes the company CFO golfing once a year, or brings the Human Resources person responsible for insurance some kind of treat— the insurance agent's informal performance appraisal is that he or she is doing a great job!

I like the insurance company advertisement that states, "Who insures you doesn't matter. Until it does." Luckily, the vast majority of businesses and individuals never have a claim—let alone a catastrophic claim. Heaven forbid that should ever happen. But what if it does? After the claim occurs is *not* the time to find out that inadequate policy limits were in place, or that you have unwillingly been self-insuring an event that could have easily been transferred to an insurance company.

So, what specifically does an insurance and risk management consultant do? Property and casualty consultants provide exposure analysis and recommendations, assist in marketing selection and implementation, and offer other specialized services as the need arises. Below are some specific services provided by a typical insurance and risk management consulting firm.

## Exposure Analysis and Recommendations

An insurance consultant, widely known within the insurance industry as a **risk management consultant**, first conducts a detailed interview with one or more key persons in the business. Key person is generally defined as the owner or a "C" level position within an organization. This interview process provides the means to identify exposures to loss and permits the consultant to recommend appropriate actions to address the exposures identified during the interview.

Risk management consultants analyze an organization's insurance and risk management programs and make recommendations regarding coverage improvements and administration, as well as loss control and financing mechanisms. Specific recommendations are provided that go beyond recommending the purchase of insurance products and that focus on areas of pure risk management. Remember that insurance is just one aspect of risk management—it is a risk transfer technique.

## Other Specialized Services

Risk management consultants also provide specialized services such as:

- claims reviews and audits
- safety program implementation and review
- litigation support and expert witness testimony
- evaluation of third-party administrators
- self-insurance analysis and captive insurance company feasibility studies
- identification of risk financing options
- insurance claims assistance
- broker and/or agent selection and review
- disaster planning implementation and review

Another way to look at an insurance consultant is as an "outsourced risk manager." Nearly all Fortune 500 companies, and many smaller ones, have risk managers on staff to perform the duties mentioned above. Smaller companies may be unable to afford a full-time risk manager but welcome assistance from a risk manager who provides services on an as-needed basis.

# 7

## Insurance Litigation

During the past several years I have become more and more involved in providing advice to attorneys, typically after a lawsuit has been filed. I have been involved on both sides of the table, plaintiff and defense, and can attest that both sides usually have a supportive argument. But know this: in most situations, insurance lawsuits come about due to a *failure to communicate* in some fashion.

Several of my cases that pertain to insurance *defense* work involve insurance agent negligence. I am hired by insurance companies that provide Insurance Agent Errors and Omissions insurance coverage to the insurance agency and to the specific insurance agent accused of some type of negligent action or inaction.

While insurance agent responsibilities vary from state to state, several states hold that it is the responsibility of insurance **buyers** to tell their insurance agents what coverages and what limits of insurance are desired. In essence, the insurance agent is charged with "taking the order" of their customer. Of course, this relationship is situation-dependent and can be altered depending on things such as the length of time the insurance customer and insurance agent relationship has been in effect, whether the insurance agent gives proactive advice and holds himself or herself out as an expert, whether fees in addition to commissions are charged, and so forth.

However, if a typical customer/agent relationship is said to exist, the insurance agent's primary responsibility is simply to order the insurance coverage that their customer tells them to order and to provide a cursory review of insurance policies after the insurance policies have been issued so that the insurance agent can determine whether or not what was ordered was delivered.

Cases that involve supporting the *plaintiffs* usually occur after there has been a series of discussions between the insurance policyholder and the insurance company claims adjuster. Many times, the insurance company determines at the onset of a claim that coverage under the insurance policy (contract) may not apply. In these situations, a **reservation of rights** letter is sent to the insured policyholder before any other action is taken by the insurance company. In these situations, insurance company defense *may or may not* be provided to the insured.

I have seen some situations where an insurance company's actions are absolutely appropriate, in my opinion. On the other hand, I have also seen insurance carriers make poor decisions (i.e., wrong coverage determinations) and then dig in their heels when there is little, if any, support for their position. In these situations, insurance companies have a built-in advantage in the legal system. They can deny coverage and as long as they have a "reasonable" explanation for their decision, they can hold onto the money that they would have paid for a claim until such time that a court determines that the claim *must* be paid.

## Bad Faith

The term **bad faith** resulted from courts holding that there is an *implied covenant of good faith and fair dealing* in all contracts of insurance. This is because insurance contracts have special characteristics—including the fact that they are **unilateral** (drafted by only one party—the insurance company) and **aleatory** (the contract is based upon the insurance company's promise to pay for a future unknown event).

The burden of proof is on the plaintiff to prove that bad faith should apply, and generally a negligence standard is applied. In other words, if a plaintiff can show that another insurer would not have reasonably denied or delayed payment of the claim under the same facts as the defendant insurer did, then the defendant insurer *may* be guilty of acting in bad faith.

States may recognize both **First Party Insurance Bad Faith** claims and **Third Party Insurance Bad Faith Claims for Excess Verdicts**. The term "First Party" refers to the insured protected by the insurance policy. The term "Third Party" refers to third party claimants who allege wrongdoing on the part of an insured—i.e., the occupant of a car who is injured when struck by an insured driver.

First Party Insurance Bad Faith claims involve an *unreasonable delay* or the *unreasonable denial* of payment of a claim. The word "reasonable" may ultimately be determined in a court of law (where oftentimes a jury is involved) based upon specific facts of the case at hand. Should an insurance company's actions be deemed unreasonable or inappropriate based on the facts of the case, a bad faith claim may be initiated by the insurance policyholder's (plaintiff) attorney.

If an insurance company has committed bad faith, then the policyholder may be entitled to one or more of the following:

- Breach of Contract Damages

- Emotional Distress
- Future Installments
- Attorney's Fees
- Punitive Damages (if allowed)

*Note:* Punitive damages are a means to punish and deter an insurance company from future similar bad acts. Some states allow punitive damages and some states do not allow punitive damages.

Depending on the state where the alleged wrongdoing took place and the specific situation involved, the application of bad faith to the cause of action may change the legal action from one based on *contract* to one based on *tort*. This change comes about because the insurance company's performance is no longer based upon the insurance contract itself, but rather the basis now becomes the breach of the implied covenant of good faith and fair dealing.

Once a bad faith tort action is initiated, the damages sought may no longer be limited to the damages that would have been owed by the insurance company under its insurance policy.

Most states impose a duty on the insurance company to exercise ordinary care (due diligence) in *all* aspects of handling claims. **Third Party Insurance Bad Faith Claims For Excess Verdicts** occur when the insured's insurance company makes payment for a claim without keeping their policyholder updated on the claim status, and when the insurance company fails to obtain input from their own insured about the claim at hand.

Many times, these situations involve "policy limits" payments, which is the limit of insurance that you paid for when you bought your insurance policy. If it appears that the total amount of payment for the claim may exceed your policy limit, then the insurance company is obligated to notify their insured (you) of this possibility because you may then become personally liable for monetary judgments above the policy's dollar limit.

Some of the duties that insurance companies must adhere to while handling claims in order to avoid Third Party Insurance Bad Faith claims include the following:

- Conducting a reasonable investigation into the facts surrounding the incident and the extent of injuries of the person making the claim against the insurance company. Based upon this investigation, the insurance company should then make a reasonable assessment as to how much money it may eventually have to pay if the case were to go to a trial.
- Advising the insured when it is probable the person seeking payment will be awarded more money than the available insurance coverage dollar limit. This allows the insured to hire their own attorney if they so choose.
- Timely and appropriately inform the insured of all settlement demands, offers and negotiations.

If the insurance company is found to have committed bad faith in this area, then the insured may be entitled to collect the following:

1. The Amount of the Judgment in Excess of the Policy Limits
2. Attorney's Fees and Costs
3. Expert Witness Fees
4. Punitive Damages (if allowed)

*Note:* In case you have missed my repetitive point, please understand that the area of bad faith can differ *dramatically* from state to state and that these types of lawsuits are always dependent upon the *specific* facts of the case at hand.

Bad faith claims are generally difficult to prove, and insurance companies are typically absolved of wrongdoing if they have a reasonable basis for their position. It is important to understand that all of my comments related to the area of bad faith are intended to be a *general* introduction to this topic. Should you desire additional information in this area, please consult with an attorney who is well-versed in this specialized area of the law.

## Sample Engagements

I mentioned at the start of this chapter that I have been involved in many insurance-related court cases. So that you might gain a better understanding of the types of things that are litigated in the insurance arena, below are examples of some cases that I have been involved in during the past several years.

### Defense Cases

- Failure of Insurance Agent to Recommend Specific Trucker's Insurance Coverage
- Failure of Insurance Agent to Provide Product Recall Insurance
- Architects' and Engineers' Professional Liability Insurance Wrongful Placement Based Upon Application Information Provided By the Business Customer
- Insurance Agent Responsibilities in the Areas of Application Completion and Issued Policy Review
- Specific Standards of Care Required of an Insurance Agent During the Insurance Application Process
- Application of Intra-Family Exclusion on a Specific Recreational Vehicle Coverage Endorsement
- Insurance Agent Responsibilities to the Insurance Carrier During the Insurance Application Process
- Insurance Agent Duties Related to Home Replacement Cost Determination

- Failure of Insurance Agent and Insurance Company to Properly Write Builder's Risk Loss of Income Coverage
- Failure of Insurance Consultant to Recommend Uninsured Coverage For Personal Vehicle Driven in Florida
- Lack of Property Insurable Interest and the Resulting Impact Upon Property Insurance Coverage
- Failure of An Insurance Agent to Submit a Customer's Directors and Officers (D&O) Claim to the Insurer
- Failure of An Insurance Agent to Submit a Customer's Employment Practices Liability (EPL) Claim to the Insurer
- Insurance Company's Claims-Handling of Their Insured's Fire Damage Claim

**Plaintiff's Cases**
- Bad Faith Claim Handling Involving Insurance Company Duty to Defend
- Denial of Water Damage Claim Within a Commercial Apartment Building and Resulting Mold Damage
- Claim Denial Due to Property Vacancy and Improper Insurance Company Interpretation of the Vacancy Condition
- Insurance Agent Failure to Offer Employment Practices Liability Insurance
- Improper Cancellation of Farm Insurance Policy
- Insurance Company Denial of a Claim for Mold Damage Within a House
- Insurance Company's Improper Denial of Their Insured's Fire Damage Claim
- Insurance Agent's Negligence In Obtaining A Business Income Insurance Policy That Lacked Requested Coverages
- Insurance Company's Failure to Offer An Appropriate Business Income Loss Settlement Amount to Their Insured

# 8

## How to Get the Best Insurance "Deal"

Insurance is confusing even to those who have made it their avocation. What can an insurance buyer do to get the *best product at the most reasonable price?* Of course, using a good consultant is invaluable to help you wade through insurance jargon but there are also common sense things that can be done by everyone—regardless of whether you have any insurance expertise.

In my opinion, one of the scariest things today is insurance sales over the internet or through direct mail when the person selling such policies has limited insurance knowledge. I have personally contacted companies that offer insurance products over the internet and through direct mail, and I have found that the representatives selling the products lack technical knowledge. Often very simple questions are confusing to them. For instance, I asked the representative to explain "automobile medical payments" coverage to me over the telephone. He failed miserably. Not only did he not explain the coverage properly, he provided incorrect information.

The main advantages of internet and direct sales methods are price and convenience. However, there are exclusive agents and independent agents who can sell at or below prices being offered over the internet or through the mail. The key is that you must find them. Certainly, the convenience of the internet and direct mail is a real factor. However, this can be countered with use of email, a fax machine or by visiting the web page of insurance agents or consultants. Go ahead and get a quote from the internet companies, but do not make an insurance policy purchase until you have completed your due diligence, which includes comparing their policy coverage and pricing to what other insurance companies offer you.

How do you go about finding a good insurance company or agent? The yellow pages and local newspaper advertising is a good place to start. Referrals are also a method of getting names; however, as mentioned earlier, you should not place too much weight on the fact that someone was referred to you. You should still interview the person thoroughly before allowing them to become your insurance representative.

This is a good place to mention a caveat. The intent of this book is not to provide a summary of a few steps that will allow you to purchase the very best insurance coverage for the least amount of money. That objective is impossible because there are too many variables at play. Situations vary from individual to individual and from business to business. Therefore, what might be best for one person's situation is not best for someone else's.

Also, understand that insurance coverages can vary considerably from insurance company to insurance company. Something as seemingly simple as "property coverage" encompasses nearly infinite differences between carriers. I have spent my entire professional career learning about coverage differences and it is simply not possible to share my knowledge about insurance policy coverages in a few sentences.

This said, there definitely are things that you can do to obtain better insurance policy pricing and improved coverages for yourself. Understand though that this will require some work on your part. One way to look at this is you may be able to save $500 by spending five hours working on your insurance program. That equates to $100 per hour for your time. Not too bad of a monetary return on time invested. The other benefit of going through the process is that you will learn new things about insurance. And more knowledge is a very good thing.

Here are specific steps that you can take to reduce the amount of money that you pay for insurance:

1.  **Prepare a summary of insurance coverages and limits of insurance that you desire for each type of insurance policy you wish to purchase.**
    For instance, if you want to obtain competitive homeowner policy quotes, develop a spreadsheet template that includes the following coverages and limits of insurance:
    *   Coverage A (Dwelling)
    *   Coverage B (Other Structures)
    *   Coverage C (Personal Property)
    *   Coverage D (Loss of Use)
    *   Coverage E (Section II Liability)
    *   Coverage F (Medical Payments)
    *   Other Coverages Desired (i.e., Flood Insurance, Sewer Backup, Inland Marine, etc.)

    A good starting place is to look at your current insurance policy to review your existing coverages and limits.

2. **Contact several different insurance agents who represent different insurance companies. Include direct writers and independent insurance agencies and get quotes from several different insurance companies.**

3. **After receiving insurance proposals it is time to begin evaluating which insurance agents and insurance companies seem likely to provide you with the best policy.**

   By now you will start to feel which insurance agency and company may best suit your situation. Things such as your initial interaction with the insurance agency, their customer service and turn-around time and pricing received all play a part in your ultimate choice. Additionally, you may want to interview the agent you will be working with in the future.

   **Some questions to ask a prospective insurance agent include:**
   * How many years have you been a licensed agent or consultant?
   * What do you consider to be your "specialty" (strongest area) and why?
   * What is your weakest area? How do you deal with that area?
   * What can you offer me that other agents cannot?
   * Who writes *your* personal insurance coverage? Many of the best agents have others write their own coverages in order to have a second set of eyes review their policies, as well as to have someone else to sue if improper coverages are written.
   * How important is continuing education to you? What is the last class you took?

* What is your opinion concerning the future of the insurance industry? Give a brief description of what you feel it will look like two years from now.
* If I do business with you, who will be handling my account— you, one of your customer service representatives or someone else in your office?
* What can I expect from you in the future? How often will you review my account? What is your renewal process?
* What types of services can you provide besides selling insurance policies?
* Provide the names and phone numbers of ten of your most satisfied clients.
* What is the best method to communicate with you— email, telephone, fax, or other?
* Which insurance companies do you represent, and what are their "A.M. Best's" ratings?
* What are the top five insurance companies you represent based upon premium volume?
* How well does the company you are proposing to write my insurance handle claims? What is their claims reputation? Are they "slow payers" or "tough payers?"

4. **Next, enter all information received into your spreadsheet. At this point you can begin excluding insurance companies, narrowing your choice down to two or three insurance companies and the agencies that represent them.**

5. **Dig deeper into the coverages provided.**
   * Ask the insurance agent you may be choosing to explain coverages that were quoted.

* Ask what differences exist between their insurance quote and what other insurance companies are offering.
* Ask the insurance agent to identify significant coverage limitations and exclusions that reduce or eliminate coverages.

**6. Choose an insurance agent and insurance company.**

**7. After you receive your insurance policies, review them to make certain that what you ordered has been delivered.**
You wouldn't believe how many errors I have found over the years when reviewing delivered insurance policies. By law in most states, you have a duty to read your insurance policies. This doesn't mean that you must have a strong understanding concerning all of the insurance policy language. It means that you need to have a level of understanding of your policy that a reasonable person in your same circumstances and with similar educational and career background would have.

Now that you know how to improve your insurance coverages and insurance policy pricing, the question remains: Will you follow through on taking these steps?

Based upon my experience more people will answer "no" than will answer "yes." Why? Most people don't want to invest the time necessary to obtain a positive outcome. Others just don't "like" insurance and would rather ignore coverages and pricing contained in their current insurance policies.

Since you have purchased this book you are more likely than the general public to give attention to your insurance policies. However, even you may feel uncomfortable with the technical aspects of insurance coverage or may not desire to spend a great deal of personal time on improving your current insurance situation.

If this describes you, there is another alternative: hire a fee-only insurance consultant.

Based upon direct feedback from clients, I can attest that insurance consultants play the role of "the great equalizer" in the insurance purchasing process. Fee-only consultants do not represent any insurance companies and work entirely on behalf of their clients. There is no dual fiduciary responsibility conflict since consultants have not signed contracts with any insurance companies.

Insurance consultants are free to recommend any insurance company that will do the best job for your specific needs. Some of the benefits realized by personal insurance and business insurance consumers when using a consultant include:

- specialized knowledge
- ability to obtain broader coverages
- ability to obtain lower prices
- time savings for client
- impartial second opinion of current insurance program, including agent and insurance company effectiveness

# 9

## Risk Management

As touched upon earlier, insurance is just one aspect of risk management—it is a risk transfer technique. Risk management is a broad discipline and its full breadth is beyond the scope of this book. However, it is important to understand some basic risk management concepts to better understand how insurance fits within risk management parameters.

A good working definition of "risk management" is attributed to Robert J. Marshburn, CRM, CIC, ARM. He defines risk management as "the practice of protecting an organization from financial harm by identifying, analyzing, and controlling risk at the lowest possible cost."

It is also important to understand where risk management and individual risk managers fit within a typical business organization. Refer to the chart below for a snapshot view of a risk management position within a corporate organizational chart.

*Figure 1: SAMPLE RISK MANAGEMENT DEPARTMENT ORGANIZATION CHART*

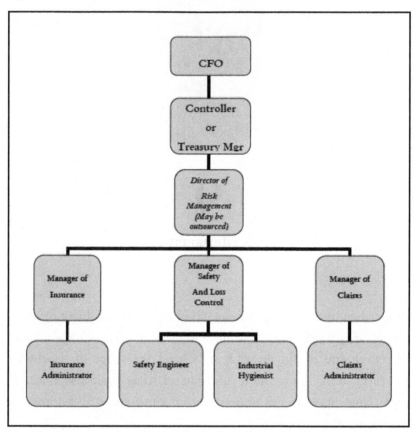

*This organization chart illustrates the structure of a typical Risk Management Department at a medium-to-large-sized company. Note: The Risk Manager can perform the duties of the positions located below his or her role, or can supervise individuals who fill these positions.*

I have also included two additional items to provide a more complete understanding of risk management. The first is a list of the risk manager's essential responsibilities. This explains the typical duties and responsibilities of a risk manager within a general business setting.

Lastly, a risk management case study has been included in the Appendix section of this book. This case study provides insight into how a risk manager analyzes a specific business situation and provides sample answers to questions related to the case study.

Keep in mind that the risk manager's *client* always makes the final decision concerning the best risk management course of action that will ultimately be taken for their specific business operations. This decision is objective for the most part, but may include some emotional or subjective reasoning as well.

For instance, I was hired as a consultant on a project for a large, complex contracting enterprise. Part of the scope of my project was to discern whether the business should have one master policy with all subsidiaries named in the master policy, or whether more than one insurance policy should be written providing coverage for one or more of the subsidiary companies.

During my project, I discovered that there was a wood furniture manufacturing business that had low revenues, high losses and seemingly no redeeming qualities. Therefore, I recommended that not only should the furniture business be written on a separate policy, I also strongly suggested that the parent corporation consider selling the furniture business.

Ultimately, the decision-maker at the parent company said that he understood the reasoning for my recommendation. The furniture business, though, happened to be founded by the parent company's majority stockholder's great-great grandfather, and it held significant sentimental value to him. As a result, they decided to make no change with regards to the furniture business.

While personally disagreeing with this course of action, I fully respected my client's decision.

## RISK MANAGER ESSENTIAL RESPONSIBILITIES

A risk manager brings a unique set of valuable skills to a company. The following list outlines the essential services a risk manager can provide:

- Researches, compiles and maintains insurance placement and renewal application underwriting information
- Negotiates and recommends the procurement, renewal, budgeting and record-keeping of all corporate insurance
- Analyzes coverage options, prepares and presents recommendations for placement
- Guides the establishment and implementation of loss control related operating and training procedures between business units and brokers/insurers
- Conducts site visits to identify risk exposures, maintains working knowledge of applicable codes and standards and recommends appropriate loss control solutions
- Manages the day-to-day risk management and insurance functions, ensuring that corporate policies are followed and amended as business needs change
- Identifies changes in corporate risk exposure. Coordinates issuance of insurance certificates
- Assists the Internal Audit Manager (or CEO, CFO, etc.), in the development and maintenance of risk management policies, procedures and programs necessary to mitigate identified corporate risk exposures
- Assist in the analysis and identification of risk exposures associated with contracts or agreements between the corporation and any contractor/vendor, including leases
- Provides risk transfer recommendations to mitigate company exposures

- Assists the Legal Department with claims management, administration and settlement
- Assists the Human Resource Department as a loss control liaison related to safety and health, medical and Worker's Compensation claim areas
- Maintains and analyzes loss experience data and recommends appropriate policy changes
- Provides corporate insurance perspectives to governmental regulatory agencies, code officials and insurance companies as required
- Represents the corporation in appropriate regulatory or public safety forums
- Performs miscellaneous ad hoc analysis as required
- Develops and communicates risk management policies
- Conducts risk identification surveys to identify risk exposures
- Arranges alternative risk financing solutions (in addition to insurance), where appropriate
- Implements/monitors loss control program
- Determines cost of risk and prepares applicable allocations to cost centers
- Participates in due diligence analysis related to mergers and acquisitions
- Designs, implements and monitors claims handling and loss control procedures
- Develops and maintains a Risk Management Policy and Procedures Manual
- Develops and maintains a Risk Management Information System to identify, measure and manage risk within the organization

- Conducts alternative funding feasibility studies to identify costs and benefits of implementing transfer mechanisms beyond traditional insurance programs. Includes analysis of alternatives such as captives or self-insurance, or joining association-owned insurance companies
- Reviews, analyzes and monitors overall Risk Management Department operations, including program results and effectiveness
- Organizes and administrates third-party self-insured provider contracts and performance
- Coordinates risk management policies with organizational mission and goals

# 10

## The Future of Insurance

Following are some of my general thoughts concerning the future of insurance.

The trend toward more government regulation will continue. Insurance represents a large part of a typical household's budget, remains confusing to those outside of the insurance industry, and concerns the public good. Therefore, it cannot and will not be ignored by lawmakers. **McCarran-Ferguson** (the law established in 1945 which gave individual states the authority to regulate their own state's insurance industry) will likely be struck down in whole or in part, and the federal government will become more active in the regulation and standardization of insurance across the United States. In fact, I initially predicted this several years ago and it has now come to fruition in the area of health insurance with implementation of the Affordable Care Act (Obamacare) currently underway.

Individual states will remain active, but they will eventually take a back seat to Washington. The federal government will continue to offer some type of legislation to safeguard insurance company assets in the event of a terrorism-related catastrophe. I made this prediction while working on my first edition of *Inside the Insurance Industry* in 2005 and again my prediction has rung true. The **Terrorism Risk Insurance Program Reauthorization Act** (TRIPRA) was passed in 2007 and extended the initial Terrorism Risk Insurance Act (TRIA) through December 31, 2014.

Easy-to-read policies made their first appearance many years ago. These should have been called "easier-to-read" policies because they are still difficult for consumers to read and understand. Insurance companies will continue to find ways to make their contracts easier to comprehend by people unfamiliar with insurance. More and more policies will be issued on a business owners (BOP) type of policy and fewer and fewer commercial package policies (CPP) will exist. This has been occurring gradually over the years as insurance companies expand their underwriting guidelines to accept higher values and a broader array of industries. Look for this expansion to continue in years to come.

Alternative distribution channels will make considerable headway in future years. People will feel more and more comfortable buying over the internet and over the telephone. Insurance will continue to be viewed as a "commodity" by consumers and price will remain the number one key consideration in the average person's decision to purchase an insurance policy. Coverages and relationship with the company and/or salespersons will become a more distant second and third place.

The trend towards "bigger and bigger" will continue. The lines between banking and insurance and mutual funds will become further and further eroded. It will become more difficult to tell the difference between the large financial services companies because all of them will offer a broad array of financial based services.

Consumers will be able to do one-stop shopping. You will have the ability to have your checking account, savings account, money market mutual fund, car loan, mortgage, brokerage account, aggressive stock mutual fund, auto/home/business insurance all at the same institution. It will be the battle of the big companies to get *all* of the consumer's financial services related business.

Eventually, with this trend towards huge financial conglomerates, there will be a backlash and resulting fallout from many customers. People will be unable to get in touch with a warm body who can answer their questions at these mega-companies. Customer service in general will deteriorate, and people will start viewing large insurance companies much like the government—as a behemoth with lots and lots of red tape, and from whom it will be nearly impossible to get a live, knowledgeable person to address their problems. In time, people will balk at their inability to access decision-makers at these large financial institutions and there will be a trend towards smaller companies again—or at least large companies that are very decentralized and that operate out of smaller regional offices.

Computers and other forms of personal technology, such as smart phones, will certainly play a more important part in the insurance industry in the future. Consumers will make use of technology to receive and to make changes to their insurance policies. Texts and emails will become the preferred method of communication between purchasers of insurance and their insurance agents and insurance companies.

Insurance companies will attempt to have computer software do more and more of the decision making and will attempt to streamline their organizations in new ways in order to save money. They will have computers recommend settlement amounts for smaller claims and will have adjusters handling only larger, more complex claims. Many years from now, computers may make nearly all claims decisions (think Watson, IBM's decision-making supercomputer). The same process will take place in the Underwriting Departments. Decisions about risk characteristics required to attain profitability will be made by computers, and underwriters will consider only the more complex submissions for insurance. Insurance companies will eventually require consumers to complete their own applications for insurance and to submit these directly to the insurance company — without insurance agent intervention or assistance.

The compensation model for insurance agents will continue to be at the forefront of discussions between insurance companies and their sales representatives. Insurance companies will want more work done by agents for less commission payment. Insurance agents will want to do less work for more commissions. There will ultimately be fewer and fewer small insurance agencies. More and more mid-size and large insurance agencies will merge to create huge insurance agency organizations that will rival the size of some regional insurance companies.

As insurance companies work more closely with their customers, the role of insurance agents will evolve. Insurance agencies may move from the role of "distributor" of insurance policies to that of "producer" of insurance policies — thereby actually competing against insurance companies for the insurance consumers' dollars. This may start with the introduction of specialized insurance products for unique or segmented businesses and will then expand into other, more standardized areas of insurance.

## Epilogue

I hope that this publication has opened your eyes and provided you with valuable information about insurance companies. If my goal has been accomplished, you are now able to protect yourself from many different types of abuses that can occur in the insurance purchasing process.

Another intent of this publication is to serve as a wake-up call to the insurance industry. There are many good people doing many good things at insurance companies. And insurance certainly does serve a vital purpose. Without insurance, there would be a tremendous strain on society, in general, as people would not be able to financially recover from catastrophes that will inevitably occur. In addition, people would spend such an inordinate amount of time worrying about "what might happen" in areas such as property or liability losses, that they would not be able to turn their attention to other worthwhile endeavors, including managing their busy lives and running their own businesses.

But I am disappointed—and ashamed at times—that my industry has not adequately addressed several important consumer issues such as truly easy-to-read policies, making pricing understandable to the public at large, sharing information about contingency commission agreements, explaining in more detail why a policy might be cancelled and helping insurance policyholders to better understand how claims frequency has a direct correlation to increases in insurance policy prices.

It is my earnest hope that insurance companies will soon feel a moral obligation to address these consumer-related areas where they are weak and will make improvements in these areas.

Let me be clear: I am proud to work in the insurance industry. Insurance allows individuals and businesses the ability to survive financial disasters by either paying claims outright or by reimbursing policyholders for situations covered under the insurance policy that was purchased. In fact, without insurance the financial stability achieved through a lifetime of savings might disappear as the result of one catastrophic event. But improvements can and should be made.

I would like to see the positive changes mentioned above implemented by insurance companies. When these changes take place, I and all who work in the insurance industry will be able to hold our heads higher and will be even more proud in the knowledge that we are associated with one of the most important and influential industries ever created.

# Appendix

Following is an example of how an insurance consultant looks at a customer's business from an insurance and risk management perspective. If you are not a business owner you may find the information that follows somewhat confusing. As a result, you may want to skip this section.

But if you are a business owner, I encourage you to put yourself in the insurance consultant's role and to spend some time going through the case study.

The consultant's crucial starting point is the identification of exposures. Next, it is important to determine how to address the exposures identified — note that insurance is only one possible way to address identified risks of loss.

As a result of completing the case study you will better understand ways to improve your business operations, as well as ways to make your company look more desirable to insurance companies.

## Western Wooden Products, Inc. Sample Risk Management Case Study

## Western Wooden Products, Inc.

Your customer is the president and CEO of Western Wooden Products, Inc. (WWP), a large privately held furniture manufacturing and repair business. They have been in business for 30 years. Sales revenues have been steadily increasing over the past five years and you now generate $150 million in annual sales and the company enjoys a healthy balance sheet.

WWP employs 250 people in the state of Wisconsin; several salespersons have offices in their homes and are located in states other than Wisconsin. One or more salespersons are located in each of the following states: Iowa, Michigan, Ohio, Minnesota, and California.

WWP has a triple-net lease in effect. The owner of WWP formed a separate company, Products Building Leases, LLC, which owns one 100,000 square foot manufacturing building that is insured on a replacement cost basis for $25,000,000. It was built in 1970, is fully sprinklered and is located in Protection Class (PC) 4. There is also a storage building that contains lumber used in WWP's manufacturing process and is located five miles away from the manufacturing building.

The title to this property is also in the name of Products Building Leases, LLC. The storage building was built in 1950 and is located in PC 10. It has 50,000 square feet and is valued on an ACV basis at $1,000,000.

Business personal property is located solely at the manufacturing facility, with the exception of lumber and several pieces of machinery and equipment, such as forklifts, which are kept at the warehouse location. The total value of business personal property at the manufacturing facility is $20,000,000 (including machinery used in the manufacturing process). Lumber located at the warehouse/storage building fluctuates in value frequently, both due to the price of lumber and to frequent inventory changes. Currently, lumber on hand is valued at $700,000 and the equipment located at the warehouse has a schedule limit of $175,000.

WWP also owns a fleet of 100 delivery trucks, 50 of which are semi-trailer and tractor units. In addition, the president of WWP owns a 2009 Mercedes Benz ML320 Bluetec SUV, valued at $50,000. It is driven mainly for personal use and is titled in the name of Western Wooden Products. The president's wife drives a 2005 Aston Martin DB9, currently valued at $75,000 which is also titled in the name of WWP.

The last private passenger auto titled in the name of WWP is driven by the president's 18-year-old son who works occasionally during the summer for WWP. He has had three speeding violations during the past three years and drives a 2003 Chevrolet Corvette Z06, currently valued at a mere $30,000.

## WESTERN WOODEN PRODUCTS
## YEAR-END FINANCIAL STATEMENT

**Income:**

| | | |
|---|---|---|
| Furniture Sales | $ 149,000,000 | |
| Excess Lumber Sales | $ 1,000,000 | |
| Gross Sales: | | $ 150,000,000 |

**Less Cost of Goods Sold:**

| | | |
|---|---|---|
| Lumber Costs | $ 75,000,000 | |
| Furniture Damaged in Mfg Process | $ 500,000 | |
| Total Costs: | | $ 75,500,000 |

**Gross Profit:** **$ 74,500,000**

**Operating Expenses:**

| | |
|---|---|
| Insurance | $ 2,500,000 |
| Utilities (Heat and Electric) | $ 1,000,000 |
| Payroll | $ 25,250,000 |
| Fixed Rents | $ 15,000,000 |
| Taxes | $ 15,750,000 |
| **Total Expenses:** | **$ 59,500,000** |

**Net Profit:** **$ 15,000,000**

## Case Analysis

1. List some of the methods you can use to identify major risk exposures to Western Wooden Products, Inc. (WWP) and Products Building Leases, LLC (PBL).
2. What are some of the techniques/tools/methods that can be used to address risk exposures?
3. What services could a risk manager provide that would help WWP and PBL address risk?
4. Identify contractual risk management tools/techniques that a risk manager may use when reviewing contracts.
5. What are some reasons for carrying a high deductible?
6. How would you go about allocating the cost of risk for both WWP and PBL?
7. Explain the concept of Enterprise Risk Management
8. What are some of the reasons it makes sense to develop a risk management policy and procedures manual

## Case Analysis

*Identify any type of exposure to loss based on the case study. Exposures may include Direct Property, Indirect Losses, General Liability, Human Resources & Employment Practices, Auto, Surety, Leases and Contracts.*

| Exposure Identified | Measurement Frequency/Severity | Recommended Treatment |
|---|---|---|
| | L M S | |
| | L M S | |
| | L M S | |
| | L M S | |
| | L M S | |
| | L M S | |
| | L M S | |
| | L M S | |
| | L M S | |
| | L M S | |
| | L M S | |
| | L M S | |
| | L M S | |

*Note:* **L** = Low, **M** = Moderate, **S** = Severe

*Used with permission of the National Alliance for Insurance Education and Research

# WESTERN WOODEN PRODUCTS, INC.

## SAMPLE RISK MANAGEMENT ANSWERS:

1. **1.List some of the methods you can use to identify major risk exposures to WWP and PBL.**

   1. Standardized surveys and questionnaires.

   2. Financial statements.

   3. Other records and files.

   4. Activities flow charts.

   5. Personal inspections.

   6. Discussions.

2. **What are some of the techniques/tools/methods that can be used to address risk exposures?**

   1. Exposure avoidance.

   2. Loss prevention.

   3. Loss reduction.

   4. Segregating exposures.

5. Contractual transfer.

6. Retention.

3. **What services could a risk manager provide that would help WWP and PBL address risk?**

A risk manager can:
*   Develop and communicate risk management policies
*   Provide communication: internal and external
*   Conduct risk identification surveys
*   Arrange risk financing (including insurance placement)
*   Manage litigation in conjunction with Claims/Legal Department
*   Investigate accidents
*   Implement loss control program
*   Provide contractual analysis and review leases
*   Determine cost of risk
*   Prepare allocations to cost centers
*   Audit existing insurance/self-insurance programs in the property, casualty, employee benefits and pension areas
*   Design insurance programs, including both primary and excess layers
*   Preparation of specifications for any and all portions of an insurance program being bid, as well as an evaluation of the responses to the specifications
*   Analyze the various funding alternatives for any particular lines of insurance to be studied
*   Participate in due diligence analysis related to mergers and acquisitions

* Design, implement and monitor claims handling and loss control procedures
* Conduct feasibility studies for captives and association-owned insurance companies
* Review, analyze and monitor overall Risk Management Department operations, program results and effectiveness
* Coordinate risk management policies with organizational mission and goals
* Facilitate the development or purchase of a Risk Management Information System (RMIS)

4. **Identify contractual risk management tools/techniques that a risk manager may use when reviewing contracts.**
   1. Hold Harmless Agreement
   2. Indemnity Agreement
   3. Exculpatory Clause

5. **What are some reasons for carrying a high deductible?**

* A credit is applied by the insurance company that lowers the price you pay for insurance.
* By carrying a high deductible you are showing the insurance company that you are willing to bear part of the risk of loss to your buildings and business personal property. This makes insurance company underwriters more comfortable with accepting your account and may result in an overall lower price for your insurance.
* Losses incurred below your deductible threshold may be eligible for deduction on your corporate federal income taxes.

## 6. How would you go about allocating the cost of risk for WWP and PBL?

* Decide whether you will use an exposure-based allocation, experience-based allocation, or a combination of the two methods
* Include the following costs in your allocation system:
    1. Risk Management Departmental costs
    2. Outside services
    3. Retained losses (passive and active)
    4. Insurance premiums
    5. Other considerations (indirect costs)

## 7. Explain the concept of Enterprise Risk Management

* Enterprise Risk Management focuses on all risks that impact the company. A good working definition of Enterprise Risk Management is "a framework for handling all of the risks facing an organization, whether insurable or not."
* Enterprise Risk Management describes an approach to risk management. It involves a wide range of tools and methodologies all designed to understand the relationship between an organization's risk profile and its impact on earnings and shareholder value.
* The four (4) main categories of enterprise risk are:
    1. Hazard/Event
    2. Financial
    3. Strategic
    4. Operational

**8. What are some of the reasons it makes sense to develop a risk management policy and procedures manual?**

The purpose of a policies and procedures manual is to:

1. Reaffirm corporate policies
2. Communicate risk management policy
3. Communicate senior management's support for the risk management program, which includes the risk management policy, the risk management mission statement, and the risk management policy and procedures manual
4. Define responsibility and authority
5. Familiarize personnel with exposures and procedures (risk management policy statements)
6. Provide a convenient reference — the "How To" guide
7. Convey a positive image of the Risk Management Department
8. Detail policies and procedures in selection of third-party service providers

# Index

**A**

accident, 20, 22-23, 38

accidents, 19, 22, 97

accommodation, 50-51

accommodations, 59

account, 19, 30, 56, 76, 87, 98

accounts, 9, 26-27, 41, 53, 56, 59

action, 13, 46, 62, 65-66, 68, 81

actions, 21, 50, 59, 63, 66-67

actuarial, 35-36

actuaries, 25, 35

Actuary, 8, 33, 35

actuary, 37

adhesion, 17

adjuster, 15, 17, 24-25, 40, 66

adjusters, 14-17, 20, 24-26, 40,
47, 61-62, 87

adjusting, 15

adverse, 8, 57

adversely, 11, 13

advice, 13-14, 62, 65-66

Advising, 69

advising, 18

advocates, 62

agencies, 3-5, 7, 11, 32, 40, 44,
55, 58-61, 75-76, 83, 88

agency, 3, 7, 9, 11, 13, 28, 37, 43,
59-60, 65, 75, 88

Agent, 65, 70-71

agent, 3-6, 9-14, 21, 24, 27-28,
30, 40, 54-56, 59-60, 62, 64-
66, 73, 75-78, 88

agents, 3-6, 9-14, 21, 24, 28, 41,
55, 65, 73, 75, 87-88

Agreement, 98

agreement, 51

agreements, 7, 49, 82, 90

aleatory, 67

ambiguities, 17

ambiguity, 42

Analysis, 63, 94-95

analysis, 26, 63-64, 82-84, 97

Analyze, 97

analyze, 35, 63, 98

Analyzes, 82

analyzes, 81, 83-84

analyzing, 79

ancillary, 34, 51

Application, 70

application, 4, 27, 58, 68, 82

applications, 14, 26, 88

Attorney, 6, 68-69

attorney, 16-17, 24-25, 28, 67,
69-70

attorneys, 15, 33-34, 40, 48, 65

Audit, 8, 28, 33, 40, 82, 97

audit, 30, 32, 40

auditable, 28-30

audited, 29

Auditors, 40

audits, 64


**B**

bias, 24

bid, 6-7, 97

bidding, 7

bids, 6

Bordereau, 51

bordereau, 50
Breach, 67
breach, 68
broad, 79, 86
broaden, 25
broader, 13, 78, 86
broker, 5-6, 12, 64
brokerage, 6, 87
brokers, 5-7, 82
Business, 29, 70-71, 92
business, 1, 3-4, 6-8, 10-13, 17-
    18, 20, 23, 25-28, 30-32,
    35-37, 40, 43, 46-47, 49-51,
    55-63, 73, 76, 78-82, 86-87,
    91-92, 98
businessowners, 41, 55


C
Cancellation, 71
cancelled, 20-21, 90
capacity, 43
Captive, 4, 11
captive, 4, 9, 64
captives, 84, 98
Carrier, 70
carrier, 7, 12-13, 28, 51, 58
carriers, 1, 3, 7, 41, 45, 61, 66, 73
Casualty, 15
casualty, 63, 97
catastrophe, 86
catastrophes, 22, 45, 49, 89
catastrophic, 19, 49, 54, 63, 90
Claim, 71
claim, 2, 13-17, 19-25, 34, 40, 45,
    61-63, 66-69, 83
claimant, 15-17

claimants, 16, 67
Claims, 8, 14-16, 18, 25, 33, 38,
    42, 67-68, 71, 97
claims, 2, 6, 14-27, 30-31, 33-37,
    39-42, 44, 47, 49-50, 61, 64,
    66-69, 76, 83, 87, 90, 98
Class, 92
class, 30, 36, 57, 75
classification, 29, 32
classifications, 29
client, 12-13, 24, 56, 78, 81
clients, 12, 30, 41, 62, 76, 78
Commercial, 29, 57, 71
commercial, 26-28, 35, 55-56, 58-
    59, 86
commission, 7, 11-12, 24, 88, 90
commissions, 6-7, 11, 13, 28, 59,
    66, 88
Compensation, 15, 29-32, 34, 39,
    58, 83
compensation, 12, 88
consult, 15, 70
Consultant, 71
consultant, 13, 17, 24, 59, 63-64,
    72, 75, 78, 81, 91
Consultants, 62
consultants, 62-64, 73, 78
consulting, 63
consumer, 2, 5, 9-10, 17, 19, 28,
    45, 52, 55, 60, 62, 87, 89-90
Consumers, 10, 19, 87
consumers, 1, 6-7, 20, 27, 45, 52,
    55-56, 78, 86, 88
contingency, 12-13, 90
contingent, 6-7, 11
Contract, 67

contract, 4, 11, 14, 17, 24-25, 41, 49, 61, 66-68
Contracts, 95
contracts, 3, 5, 9, 43, 48, 67, 78, 82, 84, 86, 94, 98
Contractual, 97
contractual, 94, 97-98
contractually, 11
Cost, 70, 93
cost, 3, 7, 17-18, 22, 24, 30, 47-48, 51-53, 59, 79, 83, 92, 94, 97, 99
Costs, 69, 93
costs, 30, 47, 52, 56-58, 84, 99
Coverage, 70-71, 74
coverage, 13-15, 17-20, 24-25, 28, 41, 53, 55, 58, 61-63, 65-66, 69, 72-73, 75, 77, 81-82
Coverages, 71, 74, 86
coverages, 6-7, 12, 16, 18, 24-25, 27, 42, 45, 60, 65, 73-78
covered, 14, 18, 25, 55, 61, 90
Customer, 70-71, 87
customer, 4, 9, 13, 16-17, 25-27, 30-31, 41, 56, 59-60, 65-66, 75-76, 91
customers, 5-7, 9-10, 12-13, 15-16, 36, 41, 46, 55, 59, 87-88

**D**
Damage, 71
damage, 16-21, 45
Damaged, 93
damaged, 20
Damages, 67-69
damages, 17, 21, 34, 38-39,

49-50, 68
defendant, 67
Defense, 70
defense, 23, 34, 65-66
Denial, 71
denial, 24, 67
denied, 20, 24-25, 67
denies, 17
deny, 16-17, 66
discrimination, 34
discriminatory, 26
distribution, 1, 3-5, 8-10, 86
distributor, 57, 88
dividend, 2, 58
dividends, 58

**E**
employee, 4, 25-26, 39, 97
Employees, 62
employees, 4, 8, 17, 25, 40, 62
employer, 18, 39, 58
Endorsement, 70
endorsement, 18
endorsements, 28, 43
exception, 26, 50, 52, 92
exceptions, 26, 55, 58
Excess, 67-69, 93
excess, 97
excluded, 50
excluding, 76
Exclusion, 70
exclusion, 18, 50
exclusions, 19, 28, 50, 77
Experience, 56
experience, 11, 17, 25, 33-34, 36, 46, 53, 58, 77, 83, 99

Expert, 69
expert, 1, 20, 64, 66
experts, 34, 51
Exposure, 63, 95-96
exposure, 28-30, 51, 54, 63, 82, 95, 99
Exposures, 95
exposures, 29, 51, 54, 63, 82-83, 91, 94, 96, 100

F
facultative, 50-52
fiduciary, 5, 9, 24, 78
fraud, 40-41
function, 28
Functions, 8-9, 11, 13, 15, 17, 19, 21, 23, 25, 27, 29, 31
functions, 9, 82
G
guaranteed, 58
guidelines, 15, 26, 34, 40, 55, 58, 86

H
Handling, 71
handling, 15-16, 19, 68-69, 76, 83, 87, 98-99
holdback, 6
homeowner, 22, 26-27, 36, 54, 57, 74
homeowners, 19, 21, 23, 35-36, 41, 55

I
IBNR, 35

identification, 64, 82-83, 91, 97
Identifier, 89
Impact, 71
impact, 8, 11, 13, 21, 33, 35, 44-46, 49, 58, 99
implementation, 63-64, 82, 85
Independent, 3, 11
independent, 3-5, 9, 13, 25-26, 33, 44, 73, 75
injuries, 19, 21, 30, 34, 38, 69
insurance, 1-31, 33-70, 72-79, 81-91, 97-98
insure, 12-13, 31, 49, 56-58
Insured, 71
insured, 20, 34, 36, 51, 57, 66-69, 84, 92
insureds, 2, 16, 33-34
Insurer, 71
insurer, 4, 12, 19, 53-54, 60, 67
insurers, 1, 21-22, 37, 41, 52-53, 82
Interest, 71
interest, 6-7, 9, 12-13, 17-18, 24, 34, 55, 58, 60-61
IRPM, 58

J
Judgment, 69
judgment, 21, 26, 29, 39, 56, 58

K
kickbacks, 40

L
Legal, 8, 33, 42, 83, 97

legal, 5-6, 9, 13, 24, 33, 38-39, 66, 68
legally, 5, 13, 19, 40
legislation, 16, 44-45, 86
liabilities, 35
Liability, 29, 70-71, 74, 95
liability, 18-19, 23, 25, 30-31, 34-36, 40, 55-57, 89
liable, 19, 21-22, 69
limit, 13, 45, 51, 61, 68-69, 92
limitations, 19, 77
Limits, 69
limits, 16, 34, 45, 63, 65, 68, 74

**M**
manufacturer, 1, 3, 12, 28, 43
Manufacturers, 3, 60
manufacturers, 1-3
manufactures, 12
manufacturing, 30, 81, 91-92
method, 3-4, 9-10, 27, 73, 76, 87
methods, 3-4, 9-10, 50, 73, 94, 96, 99
Mutual, 4
mutual, 2-3, 86-87

**N**
Negligence, 71
negligence, 38-39, 65, 67
negligent, 19, 34, 38-40, 65
negotiate, 60
negotiated, 50
Negotiates, 82
negotiations, 16, 69
negotiators, 60

**O**
occur, 19, 21-22, 31, 49, 66, 68, 89
occurred, 40
occurrence, 39, 48
occurrences, 46
occurring, 86
occurs, 14, 19, 38, 54, 61-63
Omissions, 65

**P**
Plaintiff, 71
plaintiff, 25, 65, 67
plaintiffs, 66
policies, 1, 4-7, 9-12, 16, 20, 22-23, 25-31, 34-35, 41, 43-44, 49, 51-52, 54-56, 58-59, 66, 72, 75-77, 82-84, 86-89, 97-98, 100
Policy, 6, 8, 17-18, 25, 28, 43, 69-71, 83
policy, 2, 4, 6, 8, 12-30, 34-35, 38, 41, 43, 45-47, 49-50, 52, 54-55, 60-61, 63, 66-69, 73-75, 77, 81, 83, 86, 90, 94, 100
policyholder, 15, 17-18, 20, 23, 26, 30, 33-34, 38-39, 50, 61-62, 66-68
policyholders, 2, 15-16, 19, 36, 39, 41, 52-53, 58, 90
primary, 1, 45, 50, 52, 66, 97
Process, 70, 93
process, 1, 7, 9-10, 13-14, 16-17, 19, 25, 27, 32, 36, 38, 43, 46, 51, 56, 63, 74, 76, 78, 88-89, 92

producer, 88
proposal, 7
proposals, 12, 75

**Q**
quote, 12-13, 56, 73, 77
quoted, 27, 76
quotes, 12, 53, 74-75

**R**
Rate, 35
rate, 2, 22, 27, 29, 35-37, 55-58
Ratemaking, 35
ratemaking, 27, 36
Rates, 29
rates, 20, 22-23, 25, 29, 36-37,
    41, 46, 56-58
ratio, 6, 11, 23, 56
recommendation, 42, 81
Recommendations, 63
recommendations, 30, 40, 63, 82
referral, 10
Referrals, 10, 73
referrals, 10
referred, 2, 4, 9, 35, 52, 73
Reinsurance, 49-51
reinsurance, 49-52, 56
reinsure, 49, 51
reinsured, 49
reinsurer, 49-51
Reinsurers, 49
reinsurers, 50
Risk, 15, 45, 63-64, 71, 79-81,
    83-84, 86, 91, 94, 98-100
risk, 21, 26, 29, 45, 50-52, 54-57,
    62-64, 79-84, 88, 91, 94,

96-100
risks, 21, 27, 29, 51, 91, 99

**S**
Sales, 91, 93
sales, 3-5, 8-13, 29-30, 37, 44, 55,
    57, 60, 72-73, 88, 91
salespersons, 9-10, 86, 91
settlement, 16-17, 33, 69, 83, 87
settlements, 16
Severity, 95
severity, 23, 30-31
Specialized, 64
specialized, 63-64, 70, 78, 88
Standards, 70
standards, 16, 82
submission, 26
submissions, 88
Subrogation, 8, 33, 38
subrogation, 38-40
surcharge, 22, 52
surcharges, 20
surplus, 37, 45, 50

**T**
tier, 11
tiered, 27
tiers, 55
tort, 68
Treaties, 50
Treaty, 50
treaty, 50-52

**U**
umbrella, 3, 46

Underwriter, 15
underwriter, 15, 26-27, 29, 56
Underwriters, 23, 26, 51, 58
underwriters, 15, 17, 23, 25, 27,
    35, 47, 51, 55-58, 88, 98
Underwriting, 8, 15, 18, 26, 35,
    42, 88
underwriting, 20-21, 26-27, 29,
    40, 44, 47, 52, 54-55, 59,
    82, 86
unilateral, 17, 67

Uninsured, 71

V
Verdicts, 67-68
violation, 22, 37
violations, 93

W
wrongdoing, 40, 6

# About the Author

Kevin L. Glaser is president of Risk & Insurance Services Consulting, LLC (**RISC**), a fee-only property and casualty consulting business located in Oconomowoc, Wisconsin.

**RISC** serves businesses, government entities and affluent individuals by providing professional services such as litigation support and expert witness testimony; complex insurance program design; negotiation of insurance coverages and pricing; development, implementation and monitoring of contractual risk transfer agreements; internal audits of existing insurance and risk management programs; agency and insurance company effectiveness reviews; development of unique bid templates to test the marketplace; analysis of Worker's Compensation programs, and the review of claims control practices—including evaluation of reserves and reserving practices.

Mr. Glaser began his insurance career with *American Family Mutual Insurance Group*, followed by *Fireman's Fund* and *Tower Insurance Company*, which eventually became part of the Fortune 100 *Liberty Mutual Group*.

He has worked in a wide variety of positions including: Property Adjuster; Field Underwriter; Personal Lines District Manager;

Commercial Lines District Manager, Territory Manager and Territorial Business Manager. Glaser has first-hand experience in personal lines, commercial lines, farm lines, working with affluent family accounts and providing long-term risk management services to the State of Wisconsin.

Mr. Glaser's responsibilities have included overall results for business insurance departments and personal insurance departments, as well as ratemaking and management of underwriters and support staff. In addition, he was a select member of an American Reinsurance driven, company-wide consulting project whose mission was to re-engineer GRE's existing internal company structure.

Mr. Glaser has a B.A. from Creighton University in Omaha, Nebraska, and has earned several distinguished professional insurance designations including: Chartered Property and Casualty Underwriter (**CPCU**); Certified Insurance Counselor (**CIC**); Senior Claim Law Associate (**SCLA**); Associate in Risk Management (**ARM**); Accredited Advisor in Insurance (**AAI**); Associate in Claims (**AIC**); Associate in Risk Management--Public Entities (**ARM-P**); and Associate in Insurance Services (**AIS**). He has been quoted in national news publications such as **The Wall Street Journal**, **The Milwaukee Journal Sentinel**, and **The Hartford Courant** (Hartford, CT) relative to insurance issues.

Mr. Glaser is a member of **The TASA Group, Inc.** (Technical Advisory Services for Attorneys) and is recognized as a recommended insurance expert service provider by the A.M. Best Company. Litigation support services include the areas of commercial and personal property and casualty insurance, including insurance policy review; coverage interpretations; assistance with pre-discovery strategies; review of denied claims to determine whether coverage might exist; detailed research; trial testimony and providing second opinions by reviewing key legal focus areas and identifying additional areas that may have been overlooked.

Glaser is also a faculty member of the nationally-recognized **National Alliance For Insurance Education & Research** (sponsor of *Society of Certified Insurance Counselors* courses), and is approved to teach a variety of insurance related courses related to business insurance coverages throughout the USA. Additionally, Glaser has taught insurance-related courses for the business school of the University of Wisconsin-Whitewater, which is ranked among the top 50 business schools in the USA, and has provided long-term risk management services for the *University of Wisconsin-Milwaukee.*

Community involvement includes *United Way in Waukesha County Public Policy Committee* member, serving multiple terms as Board of Directors member and president of the *Oconomowoc Area Chamber of Commerce*, and leadership roles as president and trustee of the local branch of a national non-profit organization. Mr. Glaser is former president of the *Nebraska Underwriters Association* and former vice-president of the *Business Advisors Network* (business-to-business chapter). He has been an officer of the *Oconomowoc Toastmasters Club* and has earned the Competent Toastmaster certification.

Mr. Glaser is a national speaker in the areas of insurance and risk management, presenting to diverse groups such as *Corporate Casual,* a professional association comprising accountants, attorneys and bankers; *The COSBE (Council of Small Business Executives) Group*; the *NAPFA (the National Association of Personal Financial Advisors); the MRA (Management Association); SHERM (Society For Human Resource Management);* and *TEC (The Executive Committee),* an international group of CEOs.

---

Mr. Glaser can be reached at
Risk & Insurance Services Consulting, LLC:
158 East Wisconsin Avenue
Oconomowoc, WI 53066-3034
Phone: (262) 569-0929 | Fax: (262) 569-0925 | info@riscllc.com

---

## PRODUCTS OFFERED BY
## RIGHT SIDE CREATIONS, LLC

Books:

- *Inside the Insurance Industry*
- *Inside the Insurance Industry – Second Edition*
- *Inside the Insurance Industry – Third Edition*
- *The Great Tompall: Forgotten Country Music Outlaw*


Risk Management Software:

- The **RISC** Analyzer® (Risk Management Software)

## BOOK ORDER FORM

Are you a "classic country" fan? Here's a biography you won't want to miss!

*The Great Tompall:*
*Forgotten Country Music Outlaw*
by Kevin L. Glaser
Hardcover, 6" x 9"
364 pages with more than two dozen images

Order your copy from Right Side Creations, LLC by calling 262-354-2986, visiting our online store at www.rtsidecreations.com or by completing this form and sending your check or money order by mail.

PLEASE PRINT                           Today's Date _____

Your Name _____

Address _____

City/State/ZIP _____

E-mail _____

Quantity: _____          *The Great Tompall* @ $29.95 = _____

Ship to: ☐ Same as above                    Shipping: _____

                          5.1% Sales Tax if WI resident: _____

                          Total Amt. Enclosed: _____

If shipping to a different address:

Recipient's Name _____

Address _____

City/State/ZIP _____

Shipping: $6.50 first book. $2.25 each additional book. We ship by Priority Mail within contiguous USA only. Contact us for international shipping rates or other options

Mail payment with order form to:

Right Side Creations, LLC
158 E. Wisconsin Ave.
Oconomowoc, WI 53066.

CPSIA information can be obtained
at www.ICGtesting.com
Printed in the USA
BVOW08s1943010917

493808BV00001B/35/P